Curiosities Series

KENTUCKY
Curiosities

QUIRKY CHARACTERS, ROADSIDE ODDITIES & OTHER OFFBEAT STUFF

Vince Staten and Liz Baldi

The
Globe
Pequot
Press

GUILFORD, CONNECTICUT

The information in this book was confirmed at press time. We recommend, however, that you call establishments to obtain current information before traveling.

Cover photos: Vince Staten and Liz Baldi
Text design: Bill Brown
Layout by Deborah Nicolais
Maps created by XNR Productions Inc.; © The Globe Pequot Press
Photo credits: pp. 77, 78: London-Laurel County Tourist Commission; pp. 130, 139, 163, p. 175: kentuckytourism.com; p. 156: Roy Davis, Bert & Bud's Vintage Coffins. All other photographs by the authors.

Library of Congress Cataloging-in-Publication Data
Staten, Vince, 1947-
    Kentucky curiosities: quirky characters, roadside oddities
    & other offbeat stuff / Vince Staten.
        p. cm. -- (Curiosities series)
    Includes index.
    ISBN 0-7627-2327-0
        1. Kentucky--Miscellanea. 2. Kentucky--Guidebooks. 3.
    Curiosities and wonders--Kentucky. I. Title. II. Series.

F451.6.S73 2002
917.6904'44—dc21   2002072674

Manufactured in the United States of America
First Edition/First Printing

ACKNOWLEDGMENTS

I'd like to acknowledge the people of Kentucky, past and present. This book wouldn't have been possible if Kentucky had been one of those boring states. This book also wouldn't have been possible without the help of the following people: my co-author, Liz Baldi; Jayne McClew of the Kentucky Department of Travel; Meta Marie Ball of the London-Laurel County Tourist Commission; Roy "Bud" Davis of Bert & Bud's Vintage Coffins; Bill Williams of the Louisville Slugger Museum; Bob Moody for Chicken Wolf; Tony Terry and Lane Gold at Churchill Downs; Jackie Jones of Hodgenville; Irma Raque of Kaelin's; Steve Vest and Mike Embry of *Kentucky Monthly* magazine; Jena Monahan of the *Courier-Journal;* David Jenkins, Laura Maraldo, Bruce Haney, Rod Irvin, Ronni Lundy, Larry Magnes, David Inman, Tom Jester, and Chris Wohlwend, because I always acknowledge Chris Wohlwend; my wife, Judy Staten; my editor, Mary Norris, who managed to edit this book while planning a wedding; and all the curious people of Kentucky (you know who you are).

And, finally, I'd like to acknowledge that a few towns will question their inclusion in a particular section. It was for geographic simplicity.

THE MOUNTAINS

NORTHERN KENTUCKY

THE BLUEGRASS

LOUISVILLE

THE PENNYRILE

THE JACKSON PURCHASE

CONTENTS

ABOUT THE AUTHORS

Vince Staten is a freelance writer who lives in Prospect, Kentucky. He is the author of eleven books, including the best-sellers *Did Monkeys Invent the Monkey Wrench?*, and *Do Bald Men Get Half Price Haircuts?*

A graduate of the University of Louisville, Liz Baldi has worked in journalism for two years, most recently as the best news editor to land in Henry County, Kentucky.

INTRODUCTION

HOW TO UNDERSTAND US IN KENTUCKY

When settlers from Virginia began pushing westward in the middle years of the eighteenth century, they hit a wall, literally. The Appalachian Mountains, which etched the boundary between Virginia and what would become Kentucky, seemed impenetrable.

But in 1775 a woodsman named Daniel Boone discovered the door through that wall—a gap in the mountains, the Cumberland Gap. You've probably heard about him and his discovery— it was in all the papers. When Boone and his band of thirty hearty souls crossed through that gap, they found a virgin land, completely unspoiled by human inhabitants. That was because not even the Indians would live there. Native Americans hunted on the land they called "Kentake" (an old Iroquois word meaning "the hunting grounds") and battled one another over hunting rights. But not a single Indian tribe claimed Kentucky as its home. It was just a nice place to visit and shoot deer. A lot of folks, particularly in the surrounding states, still feel that way. "Good place for hunting, but I wouldn't want to live there."

But soon many people *did* live there. The Cumberland Gap opened the way west, allowing pioneers from Virginia and North Carolina to rush into this uncharted territory and chart it. They pounded claiming stakes into the ground every hundred yards or so, laying claim to "this parcel of land that extends from the giant Oak ten steps from Grundy Creek to the tall Maple visible on the westward ridge" and to "that parcel of acreage beginning at Harmony Crossing and extending north to the fork of Owl Creek." Kentucky was soon a mishmash of competing land claims—so competing that when Kentucky was granted statehood a mere seventeen year later, in 1792, the deed map resembled a badly sewn quilt.

Kentucky's land deeds were literally a house of cards, a situation the U.S. Supreme Court recognized when it ruled in an 1809 Kentucky land dispute titled *Bodley v. Taylor:* "The very extraordinary state of the land title in that country [Kentucky] has compelled its judges, in a series of decisions, to rear up an artificial pile from which no piece can be taken, by hands not intimately acquainted with the building, without endangering the structure and producing a mischief to those holding under it."

Not even the Supreme Court of the United States understood Kentucky. The justices just threw up their hands and said, "Fellers, you all know what you did. You work it out."

The land claim mess was what drove Kentucky's founder Daniel Boone to move on. At the end of his life, embittered over getting swindled in a number of land deals, Boone left Kentucky and moved to Missouri, where he died and was buried. Of course Kentuckians couldn't allow that. They stole over to the Show-Me State under cover of darkness, asked a resident to show them where old Dan'l was buried, and spirited his ashes back to Kentucky for a proper burial. But that's a whole 'nother story, told elsewhere in this book.

Folks, it's been pretty much the same ever since. Kentucky is a land unto itself. No one in the other forty-nine understands us, or needs to—except when traveling through and seeking directions. That's when we mess with your mind: "Okay, you know where the Gulf station is? No, well, how about the Mini-Market?"

Kentucky is a curiosity, a curiosity all its own.

One day a year Kentucky is the most famous state in the Union. That's Derby Day, the first Saturday in May, when the annual Kentucky Derby is run at Churchill Downs. On that day Kentucky is the home to fast horses, beautiful women, and great whiskey.

For the other 364 days it is home to fast women, beautiful horses, and people recovering from too much whiskey.

This duality—hey, we're important today, but tomorrow we're nothing—is a perfect reflection of a state of great curiosities.

Kentucky is the home of one of the most famous persons in the world, Muhammad Ali. It is also the home of one of the most infamous, Charles Manson (his boyhood home is in Ashland—unmarked, of course).

America's first poet laureate, Robert Penn Warren, one of the most esteemed writers of the twentieth century, was a Kentuckian, as was crazy man and gonzo journalist Hunter S. Thompson.

Illinois may have Land of Lincoln on its license plates, but Kentucky was where Honest Abe was born. He just moved away rather quickly.

Curious, right? In fact, our license plate says: KENTUCKY, LAND OF CURIOSITIES. It doesn't, of course. It says THE BLUEGRASS STATE. And that's kind of curious itself. You see, bluegrass isn't blue.

These curiosities extend down to our counties: You can't buy a drink in Bourbon County (it's against the law to sell alcohol there) but you can in Christian County. Barren County is lush; Green County isn't.

The Jackson Purchase area of Kentucky wasn't purchased by President Jackson. He wasn't president in 1818 when the land was acquired from France. And while he did broker the deal, he didn't purchase the land.

Our state song, *My Old Kentucky Home,* was written by a Pittsburgh native who may have visited the state—once.

Our most famous religious forefathers were the Shakers, who immigrated to Kentucky from New England. They were a religious sect that pretty much guaranteed their own demise by preaching celibacy. There are, as you might imagine, no Shakers left, just a ghost village that's been turned into a tourist site with a lot of nice solid Shaker furniture.

We Kentuckians pride ourselves on our high moral tone, meanwhile benefiting from an economy based on smoking

(Lucky Strikes are made here), drinking (Makers Mark bourbon is distilled here), and gambling (Churchill Downs is situated here).

Our most famous export is Kentucky Fried Chicken, a fact that puzzles folks in Corbin, the hometown of Colonel Harland Sanders and home to his first restaurant. They are astonished that the world pays tribute—and lots of money—to their native son's fried chicken. They seldom ate the stuff. He was famous locally for his country ham.

Kentucky is famous for orators—from Henry Clay, the man who would rather be right than president and therefore was never president, to the two Cassius Clays, the nineteenth-century senator and the twentieth-century boxer. When asked what an orator is, Kentucky native and onetime U.S. Vice President Alben Barkley replied that it was a man who when asked what two plus two is would respond, "When in the course of human events it becomes necessary to take the second numerical and superimpose it on the figure two, then I will tell you, and I say it without fear of successful contradiction, that the consequential results amount to four."

In Kentucky we do a lot of curious things: We Kentuckians spend $30,000 on a boat to catch a $10 fish. Our monthly satellite TV subscription fees run more than our mobile home mortgage payments. We collect broken major appliances on our front porches rather than send them to the dump. We erect concrete statues of Snow White and the Seven Dwarves in our front yards.

I'd need an entire book to discuss all the curious Kentucky politicians, beginning with Kentucky native Abe Lincoln, who didn't carry the state in either of his presidential campaigns. Our politicians come by their, ahem, uniqueness honestly. What would you expect from a state where we still require politicians to swear in their oath of office that they have never fought in a duel.

We're proud of our curious history in Kentucky—so proud that we have erected 2,000 historical markers on roadsides around the state. Of course those markers don't tell you every-thing. For instance Marker 1869, which tells the story of Henry Knox, the man who lent his name to the nearby fort where all the gold is. History records that Knox rode with George Washington as he crossed the Delaware (you remember the painting). History did not record what Washington probably said to the 300-pound Knox as he boarded the boat: "Shift that fat butt, Harry—but slowly, or you'll swamp the damned boat."

That's what this book is for: to fill in the small details that didn't make the markers and help you understand what a wonder—and wonderfully curious state—Kentucky is.

So how can you hope to understand us in Kentucky?

You can't. Just enjoy our curious ways.

LOUISVILLE

LOUISVILLE

Caution: Trick question ahead.

Do you pronounce the capital of Kentucky LOOEY-ville or LEWIS-ville?

The answer will determine if you need this book or not.

No, it's not LOOEY-ville. And it's not LEWIS-ville either.

One more guess?

No, it's not LOU-a-vull, even though that's how a lot of natives pronounce the name of the state's largest city.

It's pronounced FRANK-fort!

Louisville is not the capital; it's just the largest city, the most famous city, the most prosperous city, the home of the Kentucky Derby—and the city the rest of the state tends to dismiss as "not Kentucky."

To most others in Kentucky, Louisville is a curiosity.

If you answered "Frankfort," then you may not need this book. You already know more about Kentucky than most non-Kentuckians.

WORLD'S LARGEST BAT
Louisville Slugger Museum

It looms large—and strange—over Louisville's West Main Street: a gargantuan baseball bat. To the unknowing it might seem more than curious. After all, Louisville doesn't even have a major league baseball team.

But Louisville is home to the manufacturer of the most famous baseball bat, the bat that got its name from the town, the Louisville Slugger.

This 120-foot tall bat, standing at a jaunty angle, marks the entrance to the factory and museum.

Who could swing a bat this big? Not even Paul Bunyan could take a cut with this thirty-nine-ton stick. (The

Batter up! If you strike out using this bat, better consider a different profession.

average major league bat weighs about two pounds!) It would take a man or woman at least twenty-four stories tall to wield the bat.

Inside the museum is the world's largest ball-and-glove sculpture, a seventeen-ton monument depicting a well-worn Louisville Slugger fielder's mitt holding a baseball.

Neither bat nor ball is authentic. The bat isn't ash but steel painted to look like wood. And the ball and glove were carved from a slab of 450-million-year-old Kentucky limestone.

The Louisville Slugger Museum is located at 800 West Main Street. It is open Monday through Saturday 9:00 A.M. to 5:00 P.M. and Sunday April through November noon to 5:00 P.M. Admission is $6.00 for adults and $3.50 for kids. For more information call (502) 588–7288 or check out the Web site at www.sluggermuseum.org.

DOG DAY AFTERNOON — CHICKEN WOLF

I t's easy to bemoan the decline in nicknames. When the most famous basketball player of the modern era is nicknamed M. J. (Michael Jordan) and the most famous female singer is JLo (Jennifer Lopez), it's apparent we just aren't trying. Where are the imaginative nicknames? Back in the nineteenth century, when baseball was loaded with players named Turkey (Turkey Mike Donlin) and Bow Wow (Bow Wow Arft) and Easter Egg Head (Easter Egg Head Shellenback).

There were some phenomenal nicknames for players back then (like Phenomenal Smith, a pitcher for the Phillies in 1890), but the most phenomenal nickname belonged to Jimmy Wolf. That's Jimmy "Chicken" Wolf, outfielder for the Louisville Eclipse in the 1880s.

Chicken Wolf led the American Association, then considered a major league, in batting average in 1890. But his greatest moment came on August 22, 1886. With Louisville and the Cincinnati Reds tied 3–3 in the bottom of the eleventh inning, Wolf laced a line drive toward the right field corner. The ball awakened a stray dog who had been napping in the corner of the outfield, and the mutt joined Reds outfielder Abner Powell in a chase for the ball. When it appeared—to the dog anyway—that Powell was winning the race, the canine bit into Powell's leg and refused to let go. Wolf legged out an inside-the-park home run in what could literally be called the Dog Days of Summer.

In 1886 the Louisville Eclipse played their games in Eclipse Park, at the corner of Kentucky and Seventh Streets. Wolf is buried in Cave Hill Cemetery, 701 Baxter Avenue.

MULLET CENTRAL

You go for the corn dogs! You stay for the hair fashion—or out of fashion. For one week in late August, the Kentucky State Fair is the place to go to see mullets, beehives, Big Hair, and every other out-of-style style.

Ringling may have had the Greatest Show on Earth, but this is the Greatest Show in Kentucky. Position yourself on one of the benches on the Promenade and watch. They come from all over the state, folks who might never venture outside their home county the rest of the year, and they bring with them the greatest assortment of out-of-fashion hairstyles and haircuts.

Of course there's more to the state fair than corn dogs and bad haircuts.

Head into the Main Pavilion and ask for directions to the Senior Citizen Center. Don't worry, we're not leading you to the quilting bee. Get the schedule for the annual Talking Contest. It usually attracts anywhere from a dozen to two dozen contestants. The rules are simple: The last man or woman standing and talking wins.

Each contestant is offered a chair. When the horn sounds contestants are off and talking—and talking and talking and talking. One year the fair had to hand out four blue ribbons. After two hours there were four contestants who still wouldn't shut up.

The Kentucky State Fair is held the third week in August at the State Fairgrounds just off Interstate 65 on Phillips Lane. For more information call (502) 367-5002.

Louisville Police Shoot Elvis!

When "The Pelvis" first performed in Kentucky on November 25, 1956, at the National Guard Armory, local police were so worried about riots that they filmed the entire show. In black and white. With no sound. Which seems to be against the point. Had they gone with color sound stock, a quarter century later they could have made a fortune selling the footage to David Wolper for his documentary *This Is Elvis*. Instead they got pennies for the black-and-white silent stuff.

But we are getting ahead of ourselves. What were they afraid of? That Elvis might incite teenage girls to—what? Scream? Faint? Chief of Police Henry Walker told the local newspaper that his department was concerned that Elvis might incite a riot. In the end the concert went off without a hitch.

Other Elvis connections in Louisville:

His grandfather Jesse Presley is buried here, in Plot 17 of Louisville Memorial Gardens. Jesse was Vernon's father and the estranged ex-husband of Minnie Mae Presley, who lived at Graceland and cooked many of Elvis's grilled peanut-butter-and-banana sandwiches. He was also the namesake of Elvis's dead twin, Jesse Garon. Jesse was in attendance at that 1956 show—the first time he had seen Elvis perform.

Elvis' first stalker also lived in Louisville. His FBI file contained a threatening postcard mailed from Louisville and records of threatening and harassing phone calls traced to a Louisville phone number. The caller would tell Elvis's family in Memphis that Elvis had been killed in a plane crash.

Elvis's "dangerous" 1956 show was held at the National Guard Armory, now Louisville Gardens, a city-owned auditorium located on the corner of Sixth and Muhammad Ali Boulevard. Louisville Memorial Gardens is at 4400 Dixie Highway (U.S. 31W) just south of I–264. The phone calls were traced to a phone booth outside a Convenient Market at 3356 Broadway in downtown Louisville. Take the Broadway exit from I–65, and head west for 3.2 miles.

MARVIN BARNES'S TIME MACHINE

Marvin "Bad News" Barnes was the most free-spirited of the many free-spirited basketball players who passed through Louisville in the days of the old American Basketball Association. Marvin ate McDonald's hamburgers on the bench, paraded around the dressing room in a full length mink coat with his uniform underneath, and accused his teammates of selfishness because they wouldn't pass him the ball when he had forty-eight points and needed only one basket to score fifty. In one season alone he missed more than one hundred team practices, but his most famous miss was a plane flight.

As Bob Costas, then team announcer for Barnes's team, the St. Louis Spirits, tells it in the book *Loose Balls:* "Because of the change of time zones, our return flight would leave Louisville at 8:00 A.M. and arrive in St. Louis at 7:57 A.M. Marvin looked at that and announced, 'I ain't goin' on no time machine. I ain't takin' no flight that takes me back in time'."

You can't go back in time anymore, but you can travel at the speed of time. Southwest Airlines' schedule from Louisville to St. Louis lists most flights arriving ten minutes after their departure. But if you travel at 8:30 A.M., you can arrive in St. Louis at 8:30 A.M.

What would Marvin Barnes think of that?

Louisville International Airport is located at the intersection of Interstates 65 and 264.

TEN ROUNDS WITH THE QUOTABLE MUHAMMAD ALI

1. "It's hard to be humble when you're as great as I am."
2. "It's just a job. Grass grows, birds fly, waves pound the sand. I just beat people up."
3. "I was the Elvis of boxing."
4. "I was so fast that I could get up, cross the room, turn off the light, and get back in bed before the light went off."
5. Before fighting Archie Moore in 1962: "Don't block the halls/And don't block the door/For y'all may go home/After round four."
6. "Howard Cosell was gonna be a boxer when he was a kid, only they couldn't find a mouthpiece big enough."
7. "Service to others is the rent you pay for your room here on earth."
8. "Prejudice comes from being in the dark; sunlight disinfects it."
9. "The man who views the world at fifty the same as he did at twenty has wasted thirty years of his life."
10. "The man who has no imagination has no wings."

WORLD'S ONLY STEAMBOAT RACE

There is only one rule in steamboat racing: There are no rules. So when the *Delta Queen* arrives at Louisville's waterfront each April to race the smaller but feistier *Belle of Louisville,* anything goes.

The two tourist boats race from the downtown bridge to Twelve Mile Island and back, a race that usually consumes a couple of hours. It's not exactly thrill-a-minute action. But the revelers on the boats and on the shores don't notice. For them it's just an excuse to party.

The winner receives a set of mounted deer antlers, not much of an incentive for two hours' labor. But the antlers aren't the important thing; bragging rights are. The antlers seem to go back and forth, leading some local wags to suggest that all is not on the up-and-up.

Whether the Great Steamboat Race is the Ohio River's answer to professional wrestling hasn't been proved. But regardless of whether the fix is in or not, locals sure engage in some shenanigans to help the local favorite win.

One year as the *Belle* and the *Queen* arrived neck and neck at the upper river turn, a pair of speedy tugs raced from the underbrush and helped the *Belle* make her turn, leaving the larger, heavier *Queen* to huff and puff to reverse course.

If you come, bring a stocked cooler.

There are numerous vantage points on both the Kentucky and Indiana sides of the river from which to watch, but the best viewpoint is on board. *Belle of Louisville* tickets invariably sell out. You can usually walk up and buy *Delta Queen* tickets for $50 per person at Waterfront Park, located at the foot of First Street on the Ohio River. For information on the *Belle of Louisville* call (502) 574–2355. From out of state call (866) 832–0011. The *Delta Queen* is currently in bankruptcy. They still accept reservations at (504) 586–0631.

QUINTESSENTIAL KENTUCKIANS

Mike Barry—The Original Louisville Lip

*T*hey invented the word "ornery" for Mike Barry. Also the word "plucky." Barry, a longtime Louisville journalist and columnist, never met a community icon he couldn't kick in the shins.

Barry began his journalism career while still in his teens, writing a sports column for his father's paper, The Kentucky Irish American. He took over the paper in 1950 and did everything from writing front-page headlines to setting type. He loved the work but the pay, that was another matter. He had to take side jobs to keep his six children fed and clothed. He told the Kentucky Oral History Project, "At one time, I was doing the Kentucky Irish American *every* week, a weekly column for the Louisville Times, and a daily radio show, being an odds maker for all the Kentucky tracks, and working the Kentucky Thoroughbred Breeders Association job."

He folded his newspaper in 1968 and became a full-time columnist for the Louisville Times. It was at the Times that he established his reputation for an acerbic wit. He was not a fan of the sportswriter as fan and went out of his way to chide writers who "fell in love" with the teams they covered. "If you're a sportswriter, you never become a cheerleader," he said.

He also disliked the way local sportscasters referred to the Cincinnati Reds, located a hundred miles and a state away, as "our Reds." In his column he created the Reds Are My Second Choice fan club. "Anybody else is my first choice." He especially disliked the intense awe local sportswriters held for the beloved state basketball team, the University of Kentucky Wildcats, once writing that if Kentucky were to play the Russian National Team he wouldn't know whom to root for.

It wasn't just sportswriters who suffered from his withering remarks. His own editors were also targets. He once said of a Louisville newspaper big shot, "I think he ran away enough good men to staff four metropolitan papers."

Barry wrote about all sports but saved his greatest affection for horse racing. He was an inveterate bettor who claimed to have seen his first Kentucky Derby in 1922 at age twelve and to have missed the event only while serving overseas during World War II.

When he closed the Irish American he donated the newpaper's files to the University of Louisville Library, which stored them in the rare book room. Barry claimed to be baffled, telling the Oral History project, "I thought a rare book was one that paid track odds."

WORLD'S LARGEST MULES

Yup, we got 'em. Or had 'em anyway. Big 'uns too. Why the biggest 'un, Apollo, stood 19.1 hands high—which for you city folk is about 6 feet, 6 inches tall. That's at the rump. You don't measure mules like basketball players. His head was a whopper, too, measuring 34 inches long. Apollo and his buddy, Anak—mules are sterile, so there was no romantic interest there—were the two largest mules in the world according to the Guinness Book of World Records.

Apollo was born in 1977 and weighed in at 2,200 pounds. Anak, older by one year, weighed a hundred pounds shy of a ton and stood 18.3 hands high—a little over 6 feet tall. His head alone measured 32 inches long. Anak and Apollo went to Mule Heaven in 2001, just a few months apart. We sure miss 'em.

BULLETS OVER BULLITT COUNTY

You can hear it long before you arrive: The sounds of rat-a-tat-tat and kaboom echo from the distant valley, a sign you are on the right road. It's the annual Bullitt County Machine Gun Shoot and Military Gun Show, and gun enthusiasts from both coasts arrive via motorcycle and RV for a chance to try out some of their heavy artillery.

You are liable to see just about any legal weapon, and a few that barely skirt the fringes of the law—not just rifles that would drop an elephant but also machine guns, infantry rifles, even bazookas. A serious shooter can go through a hundred-dollar ammunition clip in a heartbeat. And if you hang around long, you soon won't be able to *hear* your heartbeat.

Participants fire away at barrel drums, refrigerators, even old pickup trucks, reducing the targets to unrecognizable rubble.

This is, after all, the state that gave America Daniel Boone. Don't forget your ear protectors.

The Bullitt County Machine Gun Shoot and Military Gun Show is held in early April and early October each year at the Knob Creek Gun Range, 690 Ritchey Lane, West Point, Kentucky, 1 mile off of Dixie Highway on Highway 44. For more information call (502) 922–4457, or visit the Web site at www.knobcreekrange.com/.

AND DOWN THE STRETCH THEY COME

The history of the Kentucky Derby is the history of great horses—Citation, Whirlaway, Secretariat. But it is also the history of some equine curiosities, including The Great Redeemer and Big Al's Express.

Redeemer was a big horse, only a half hand smaller than Secretariat, but he was more Clydesdale than sprinter, and he's the reason a horse now has to qualify. Redeemer had no business running against the best three-year-olds, but business was what got him in the Derby in 1979: His owner paid the entrance fee of $50,000, and Churchill Downs officials allowed him to be the twenty-third horse in the field. He broke slow and stayed slow. The traditional winner's photo was a wide angle shot: As Derby winner Spectacular Bid crossed the finish line, The Great Redeemer could be seen making the turn—a quarter mile behind in a mile-and-a-quarter race. Every five steps that Bid took Redeemer fell one back.

Big Al's Express was a dream horse, the dream of California farmer Al Nesbitt, who had always dreamed of running a horse in the Kentucky Derby, even though he had no experience as a breeder or trainer. He bought a feisty Thoroughbred named

*Talk about horsepower. Experience the fastest two minutes
in sports at the Kentucky Derby at Churchill Downs.*

Lucifer's Express, renamed him after himself, and headed cross
country with the horse riding behind his old Buick in a single
horse trailer. The Buick gave it up in St. Louis, but Al found a
friendly soul who helped him get Express to the track.

Local sportswriters were waiting; they'd been hearing the
Big Al saga for days from their counterparts on the path of the
Buick. Big Al's Express looked good—shiny coat, attentive
eyes. There was only one problem. He had never raced before.
Officials told Nesbitt that he could enter his horse in the 1983
Derby, but first the horse would have to prove he could start
from a gate. Three days later Big Al's Express was still shying
away from a gate position. Finally Derby officials let Nesbitt
run the horse from a standing start in a maiden race. To every-

one's surprise the Express took off, leading the field at the first turn. But it was not to be. The horse faded to last, dead last, 45 lengths back, and Big Al and Big Al's Express reluctantly gave up their dream and headed back to California—in their Buick.

But it was a great dream, one seized on by many track regulars, who are but dreamers themselves.

Churchill Downs is located at 600 Central Avenue. Take exit 9, Southern Parkway, from I–264 and follow the signs to the Downs. For more information call (502) 636–4400 or visit www.churchilldowns.com.

THERE'S BUTTONS ON THAT BAER

I t calls itself the World's Largest Button and Fabric Store. And if you were to see all the buttons this downtown icon has, you'd believe the hype. Baer Fabrics is a seamstress's dream: three floors— 95,000 square feet of patterns and fabric, buttons and bows, sergers and sewing machines, quilting and trim. Baer's even has aiglets, something most people don't even know how to spell, much less what they do. (They're the sheath over the end of your shoelace. But in the sewing world they have many uses.)

You can find buttons as big as your Buick at Baer Fabrics.

Baer's was founded ninety-five years ago by Abraham Baer, and it's still in the family. Baer's granddaughter Linda Goldberg and her husband, Stuart, now operate the shop, although shop makes it sound quaint. It's not quaint, it's huge.

Baer Fabrics is located at 515 East Market Street; (502) 583–5521.

MORE FUN THAN A BARREL OF ANTIQUES

If you're in need of a 10-foot-tall toy soldier, you've come to the right place. Joe Ley Antiques has one. In fact Joe Ley has just about anything you could possibly use to decorate your home—and quite a bit that you couldn't. Architects and builders from all over flock to Joe's to peruse his more than 5,000 old doors; hundreds of mantels, balconies, and gates; and architectural ornaments of all shapes, sizes, and colors.

Joe Ley even has a category of merchandise the company calls "Monkey Decor." Want a monkey candleholder? Got it. Monkey cardholder? Got that, too. Even got a monkey sphere

From monkey décor to more than 5,000 old doors, everything's for sale at Joe Ley's Antiques . . .

. . . except the cars parked outside.

holder (a statue of a monkey on his back, holding a globe with his hands and feet; it'll set you back $20).

At this writing Joe has in his possession an 8-foot-high cast aluminum Statue of Liberty, perfect for the hostess who has everything.

All the merchandise—and it changes constantly—is spread throughout a hundred year old schoolhouse, which offers two acres of display space.

Fabulous would be the word to describe much of Ley's collection of collectibles. More than 100,000 visitors a year walk through; in fact Joe has had to institute an admission fee (albeit a nominal one of $1.00) to keep out the gawkers.

Joe Ley Antiques is located at 615 East Market Street, just 1 block east of Baer Fabrics. Call (502) 583-4014.

DR. GONZO BORN HERE

*T*he creator of "gonzo" journalism, Hunter S. Thompson, a.k.a. "The Doctor," hails from Louisville. Yes, the man known more for his hard lifestyle—heaving drinking, drug addiction, and being the first journalist to party like a rock star—was born and raised by his librarian mother in the Cherokee Park area. Oddly it was a story Thompson wrote about the Kentucky Derby that would catapult his career in journalism. Never mind that he made the entire thing up.

After graduating from Male High School, Thompson joined the Air Force in 1955 as an electronics expert. Although he had never written anything before, Thompson had always had an interest in books and writing, including serving as an officer of the Athenaeum Literary Association while at Male High. Not entirely interested in electronics, Thompson decided to try his hand at writing. He sent the editor of the Eglin Air Force Base paper, Command Courier, a story he wrote about the Kentucky Derby. He was hired as the sports editor, and the topic of the Derby would recur throughout Thompson's career.

Thompson grew tired of the Air Force and decided to pursue a career in journalism. In October 1957 he received an honorable discharge and moved to New York City, where he took classes at Columbia University. Thompson soon got a job at Time as a copy boy and was delighted at his salary of $50 a week.

Thompson's career took off, and in 1960 he began working in Puerto Rico for El Sportivo, *a magazine dedicated to bowling, of all things. In 1967 Thompson published his first book,* Hell's Angels, *about his experiences traveling with and being beaten up by members of the motorcycle gang. Two more publications brought Thompson into 1970. The first was an article that ran in* Scanlan's Monthly *called "The Kentucky Derby Is Decadent and Depraved," where Thompson wrote, "Take my word for it folks, I have gone to the Kentucky Derby nine or ten times in a row, and I still have recurring nightmares about it that cause me to wake up sweating and screaming like some kind of pig being eaten alive by meat bats." The other coup for that year was the acclaimed narrative of his quest for the American Dream, "Fear and Loathing in Las Vegas," which was made into a movie in the late 1990s starring Johnny Depp, another Kentucky native.*

After this Thompson focused on politics with Fear and Loathing: On the Campaign Trail of '72. *His collection of ramblings,* The Great Shark Hunt, *explored Thompson's "distrust of anyone standing under red, white and blue bunting." In the mid '70s Thompson took a turn on the other side of politics, running for sheriff of Aspen, Colorado. He lost—but garnered more media attention than any other candidate for the sheriff's office.*

Thompson took a minibreak from writing in the late 1980s. He was lured back by modern technology and currently writes for ESPN.com covering a variety of subjects, including—of course—the Kentucky Derby.

Almost Menlo Park

W e coulda been a contender. Young Thomas Edison (he was nineteen) moved to Louisville in 1866 to work as a telegraph operator because the city was experiencing a shortage of such then. He settled in a small house in Butchertown, the meat-processing district, where he tinkered on plans for improvements to the telegraph. He didn't patent anything while living in Louisville, but he did spill acid on the floor of the Western Union office while experimenting on a new kind of battery. The acid

Probably safe to say that many bright ideas were born here, at
Thomas Edison's Louisville home.

leaked through the floorboard onto his desk, and he was fired the next day. He burned his desk in a rage, taking the next train northeast to Boston, where he would soon be issued a patent, the first of 125, for an electrical vote recorder.

We don't begrudge him leaving us and creating his scientific lab at Menlo Park in New Jersey. In fact we celebrate him with the annual Edison Birthday Celebration, held the first week in February at the Thomas Edison Museum, a tiny exhibition in his old house. The highlight is a display of light bulbs. There are also exhibits of proposed inventions from local elementary school students who hope to emulate Edison, at least in the inventing part, if not in the leaving Louisville in a huff part.

The Thomas Edison Museum is located at 729–31 East Washington Street. From I–64 take the Story Avenue exit (exit 8). Turn right at the first light onto Adams Street and follow Adams to East Washington. Turn right and go 7 blocks. Hours are Tuesday through Saturday 10:00 A.M. to 2:00 P.M. Admission is $2.00. For more information call (502) 585–5247.

JUST A FRONT

It may be true, as the 1964 Dionne Warwick hit goes, that a house is not a home. But when it comes to the Charles Heigold House in Louisville, it isn't even a house. It's just a front—a facade that has somehow managed to survive tornadoes and floods and even the wrecking ball.

It has one other claim to fame: It is also the only known monument to President James Buchanan. You remember President James Buchanan. Old Tippecanoe; no that was William Henry Harrison. Old Ironsides; no, that was a boat. Old Buck, that's it, that's what they called him. You do remember from junior high history that he was president, don't you?

Facade, sweet facade.
The Charles Heigold
House is the only known
monument to President
James Buchanan.

And he has a monument, thanks to German immigrant Charles Heigold. Wanting to express his love for his new country and city, Heigold carved patriotic expressions into the front facade of his house. It just so happened that the rather boring Buchanan was president at the time. Not to worry, some of the nationalist sayings he carved include "Hail to Buchanan now and forever!" "All hail to the city of Louisville!" "The Union forever, all hail to this Union, let us never dissolve it."

The house was originally located on Marion Street. However, due to construction the house was slated for the landfill until Mayor Charles Farnsley rescued the facade and had it relocated to Thurston Park on River Road.

Aside from being the only monument to Buchanan, the facade has received national acclaim. It has appeared in Liberty Bank commercials as a national symbol of patriotism.

The Charles Heigold House is on River Road, just west of Zorn Avenue.

Row, Row, Row Your Boat

*A*t its widest the Kentucky River is barely a hundred yards across. And the Ohio River, which forms Kentucky's northern border, is less than a mile across. That's why when Louisville native Tori Murden decided she wanted to row, she had to head to the east coast. Murden didn't have a little Sunday picnic in mind. She really wanted to row—across the Atlantic Ocean. And she did. In 1999 Murden became the first woman to row the Atlantic alone, an eighty-one-day trip that began in the Canary Islands off the coast of Africa and ended 3,333 miles later at Guadeloupe in the Caribbean.

Of course it was no average rowboat, not the kind you rent in the park. It was a sleek, high-tech model with global positioning equipment, a satellite dish, and a computer so that Murden could file a diary on the Internet. How did she do it? "One stroke at a time, one step at time, the impossible is easy to achieve," she said upon her return to dry land. Murden had proposed to Mac McClure over her satellite phone while in the middle of the Atlantic and married a month after her famous row. All together now: Sigggggghhh.

NATIONAL FARM MACHINERY SHOW AND TRACTOR PULL

They come from all over: Big Sky cattle ranchers, Southwest sheep men, Carolina tobacco farmers, Northwest apple growers. Farmers of every stripe arrive in Louisville every February for the National Farm Machinery Show, the largest indoor farm show in the country. (Have you heard of any others?)

They examine the latest in tractors, scrutinize advances in combines, kick the tires on mowers, and in general talk that back-fence talk that farmers swap when they meet on the back forty.

And then they go out on the town, too. Farm Machinery Show weekend is money in the bank for Louisville's restaurants and nightclubs. Restaurant owners grin ear-to-ear at the mention of the Farm Machinery Show. Some restaurants even have to import servers to keep up with the demand. Then the next morning it's up bright and early to ooo and ahh over the latest in milking machines.

Did I mention that the wives stay back home and tend the farm?

The National Farm Machinery Show is held at the Kentucky Fairgrounds, exit 12 off I–264. For more information call (502) 367–5004 or visit www.farmmachineryshow.org.

OLD ROUGH AND READY

In the early 1990s a rumor—fueled by a newly published book, of course—swept through historical circles. Zachary Taylor had been poisoned. Yes, Old Rough and Ready, so nicknamed because of his slovenly appearance, had died only sixteen months after assuming the presidency. Had he been murdered with arsenic by his enemies, in particular angry slave-owners? That in itself would be enough to get presidential historians up in arms, but there was a back-story. If Taylor had been poisoned, that meant Lincoln wasn't the first president to be assassinated—and that had Lincoln scholars up in arms.

There was only one solution—dig him up. The body of the former president was exhumed, after much teeth gnashing and public debate, and sure enough, he died of gastroenteritis, just like they always said. He'd been done in by a bowl of cherries and a glass of buttermilk.

Here lies Old Rough and Ready—done in by a bowl of cherries and a glass of buttermilk.

They put him back in his grave in Zachary Taylor National Cemetery, 2109 Brownsboro Road. From I–264 take exit 22, then turn west on U.S. 42. The graveyard—that's what we generally call cemeteries in Kentucky—is 0.5 mile down on the right.

HOME OF THE EDSEL

It is generally recognized as the ugliest car ever built, a guppy-faced monstrosity that makes even the AMC Gremlin seem merely homely. It is, of course, the Edsel, a Ford auto named for Henry's beloved only son, who died at age forty-nine in 1943.

Ford introduced the Edsel to an unsuspecting public in the fall of 1957. There was much fanfare, but the Edsel was met with resounding silence. People whispered about that puckered-up grill and that ugly protuberance that ran along the side, an oblong boil some called the side trim. A few people bought them—very few. After three production years Ford mothballed its ugly stepchild.

Today the Edsel is a collector's item, fetching thousands of dollars because of its rarity. But it's still an ugly, ugly car.

Every Edsel was manufactured at the Louisville Ford Plant on Fern Valley Road. Take the Fern Valley Road exit off I–65 and head west. It's the big, ugly, industrial-looking plant.

THINKING IN LOUISVILLE

H e's the original wise guy—sitting on his pedestal, pondering the fate of the world or the disaster that was his most recent blind date—or why his creator, sculptor Rodin, didn't give him any clothes.

I think, therefore I am. An original cast of Rodin's famous statue, lost in thought at the University of Louisville.

He is *The Thinker,* one of the most famous statues in the world. There are hundreds of copies in souvenir shops but only twenty-five original casts, and one of them is at the main entrance to the University of Louisville's campus. And this is the only cast made using the original "lost-wax" method, which dates to antiquity.

Rodin's original was a mere 27 inches high. An over-life-size enlargement was created for a Paris exhibition. The first large bronze was cast not by the artist but by A. A. Hebrard in 1904 for the Louisiana Purchase Exposition in St. Louis. Rodin rejected it, and it ended up at the University of Louisville.

The Thinker is in front of the University's administration building, Grawemeyer Hall. From I–65 exit at Arthur Street; head west on Cardinal Boulevard, then south on Third Street a half block to the university entrance.

THUNDER OVER LOUISVILLE

You probably thought it was the Fourth of July fireworks at the Washington Monument—or maybe Disneyland. But the world's largest fireworks display is Thunder Over Louisville, an annual street party that kicks off Louisville's Kentucky Derby Festival.

There was a time when the Kentucky Derby was the only attraction at Derby time. Then the city fathers added a parade, followed soon by a steamboat race, and pretty soon it was a weeklong festival. As more and more events piled up—bike runs, minimarathons, quilt festivals—it became Derby Week. It wasn't long till they couldn't contain all the celebrating in a seven-day period. That's when it became the Kentucky Derby Festival, a two-week celebration.

To kick it all off they introduced a giant fireworks show, held on the banks of the Ohio River, with a half-million dollars' worth of firecrackers going off over a half hour period. It is spectacular, a sight worthy of comparison with the opening ceremonies of the Olympics.

You want numbers? Try 60 tons of fireworks, 250 tons of launching tubes, two million pounds of sand to pack the firing tubes, 700 miles of wire cable connecting twenty firing boards, and 1,800 feet of barges to use for a firing platform. And they set it all to music.

Thunder Over Louisville is held on the Saturday two weeks preceding the Kentucky Derby—which is the first Saturday in May—at the intersection of I–65 and the Ohio River. For information call the Kentucky Derby Festival at (502) 584–6383. You'll probably have to park at least a mile away and walk to the riverfront—but, hey, it's free.

"*L*" Is for *Louisville*

*S*ue Grafton, mystery novelist, was born in Louisville on April 4, 1940. Grafton grew up down the street from fellow writer and Louisville native Hunter S. Thompson. When Grafton was in the third grade and Thompson in the sixth, he and his cousins use to "torture" her in front of the local drugstore by riding their bikes along the back of her shoes as she walked by.

Grafton somehow made it out of the neighborhood and through the University of Louisville. She left Kentucky and moved to California in 1961, settling in Hollywood and working for fifteen years as a screenwriter. In 1982 she began her popular detective series with A is for Alibi. Her books have been translated into more than twenty-four languages.

Grafton decided to return to Kentucky after her book L is for Lawless, which takes series heroine Kinsey Millhone to Louisville. Grafton and her husband purchased a Tudor style home off River Road, where they live for four months out of the year.

TED BUNDY HAD COFFEE—AND THAT'S ALL—HERE

After breaking out of jail in Colorado, Ted Bundy stopped in Louisville for a bite to eat on his way to Florida. Bundy later said that he chose Florida because he wanted to get caught in a state that had the death penalty so that he "couldn't hurt anyone, anymore." After being caught, he would later recant and claim he was innocent. Then he claimed that he did kill all those people and more but would only tell additional details if authorities agreed to give him extra time before his execution for each victim he confessed to. In the end he got his due.

Bundy claimed that he didn't kill anyone in Louisville, and local law enforcement officers say they have no cold cases from the day he was in town. When asked if he killed anyone here, he smiled and said, "I wasn't in town long enough."

Ted Bundy had coffee at Kim's Coffee Shop, 1704 Rowan Avenue. From I–64 take Twenty-second Street to Rowan and turn east.

WHERE TACKY IS A TRADITION

There are two kinds of tacky. There's the sad kind, where the host doesn't know that Velveeta isn't really an hors d'oeuvres cheese and that shag carpet is no longer cool. And there is the fun kind, where the host is playing along with the gag and everyone knows it's okay to laugh. Lynn's Paradise Cafe is the second kind: a fun establishment that's home to great food and great kitsch.

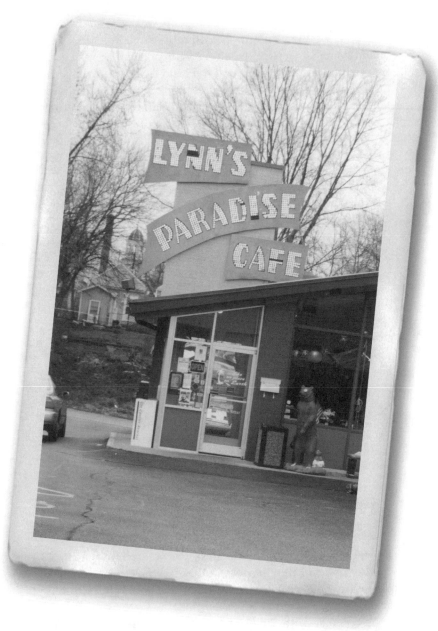

Bringing kitsch to a higher level. To find Lynn's Paradise Cafe, take a right at the giant purple cow.

Take the table settings—not literally, of course, then Lynn's would be missing part of its personality. There are the adorable little salt and pepper shakers, the kind Grandma used to bring back from Florida and mom would hide as soon as Grandma left. There are the hideous centerpiece lamps, the kind that Uncle Frank would send as anniversary presents. And there are the tables and chairs themselves, all retired dinette sets, rescued from a residence where the fifties never ended. Lots of chrome, lots of Formica, lots of Naugahyde—and lots of fun.

Plus lots of food. That's a Lynn's specialty: hardy portions that only a lumberjack could finish off. Like bacon and fried potatoes and heavy omelettes? You'll win with Lynn. If you can eat only one thing, order the "Country Ham Eggstravaganza," a country ham steak and three eggs. You won't need to eat again all day.

Lynn's is also home of the Ugly Lamp Contest. What started as a goof—bring in the ugliest lamp in your house and win a free breakfast—is now an annual tradition.

Lynn's Paradise Cafe is located at 984 Barrett Avenue. From I-264 take exit 16, Bardstown Road, north. Go left on Grinstead and right on Barrett. You can't miss it. There's a giant purple cow and a giant coffee cup out front. You can call (502) 583-3447 for reservations, but you don't really need them unless there's a bunch of you.

WHO MOVED THE CHEESE?

If you're looking for the rat race, you've come to the right state. In Louisville there's the Run for the Roses, the nickname for the Kentucky Derby, and then there's the Running of the Rodents. It's a real rat race.

To coincide with the Kentucky Derby Festival—and to have a little fun—the students at Spalding University created the

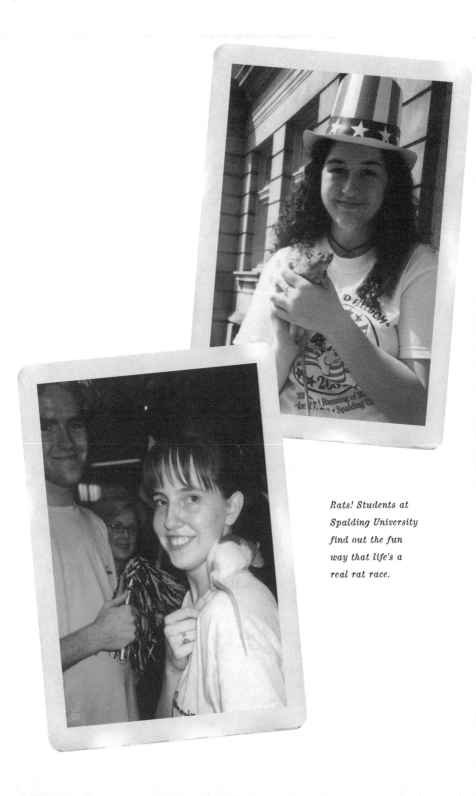

Rats! Students at Spalding University find out the fun way that life's a real rat race.

rodents race, which combines the competitive spirit of Kentucky Derby with the academic regimen of biology lab, where white-coated professors run rats through the maze. Student-trained rodents go head-to-head against other student-trained rats in a two-lane maze. Winners move on in the competition. Losers go back to being lab rats.

It takes a couple of hours for the dozen or so rodents to make it to the final round, but when they do the brass band comes out, and a crowd gathers to watch the Big Moment. We love a rat race, don't we?

Spalding University is at 833 South Third Street. From I–65 take the Broadway exit. Head west on Broadway and then south on Third. There's no charge to watch the race. For more information contact Spalding University at (502) 585–9911, ext. 2422.

HOT ROD REDUX

Science has created an expression for the phenomenon of pot-bellied men driving souped-up roadsters on main highways. It's called midlife crisis, and it's on full display every August at the National Street Rod Association's Annual Car Show held at the fairgrounds. These middle-aged men—and participants are 99 percent male—take over the city's streets. You'd think you were back in the fifties from all the candy apple–red '55 Chevy's and Ford Fairlane's with flame jobs painted on the side.

Mufflers that would get a high school kid a week's worth of detention are admired at this event, where more than 5,000 hot-rodders from across the country relive their adolescence for one weekend, competing in four categories and seven divisions. There's no category for loudest muffler, but if there were, you can bet there'd be plenty of entries.

It's easy to find the Hot Rod Show. Just head to the intersection of I–65 and I–264, roll down your window, and listen for the revving sounds. The show is held the first weekend in August. Adult admission in recent years has been $12 per person. The show will be held in Louisville at least through 2010. For more information contact the NHRA office in Memphis, Tennessee at (903) 452–4030.

THE BIRTHPLACE OF CHEWING GUM

*H*e called it Colgan's Taffy Tolu, and if that name had stuck we probably wouldn't be writing this capsule today. But fortunately wiser heads, and naming instincts, prevailed, and chewing gum *entered the language and the culture.*

In the years after the Civil War, Louisville pharmacist John Colgan noticed children peeling sticky sap from tree bark and chewing it. He knew there had to be a better way—tastier and more hygienic. So in 1879 he began experimenting, eventually turning to a medicinal gum called Myroxylon Balsamum, which was used in ground-up form in a number of medicines.

Taffy Tolu had a strong, pungent flavor, but kids seemed to love it. He began marketing the Taffy Tolu in a stick form, and it took off. In 1890 he sold his pharmacy and went into gum production full time. But the real watershed moment came when he sold Taffy Tolu at the 1893 Chicago's Worlds Fair. It was a smash. A fairgoer named Wrigley noticed Colgan's success and began his own experiments, tests that led to Chicago and Wrigley Gum becoming the epicenter of chewing gum and poor John Colgan fading back into obscurity.

CHEESEBURGER PARADISE

Irma Raque admits that her family's sixty-five-year-old restaurant may not be THE inventor of the cheeseburger, but she says it was one of the inventors. "I'm sure other restaurants tried it about the same time. But when Daddy put cheese on a burger back then, he'd never heard of anyone else doing it."

Daddy was Carl Kaelin, and his fortuitous pairing of hamburger and cheese was a fluke occurrence. Kaelin was heading to the local food distributor for his daily pickup when he stopped by the kitchen to tell his wife, Margaret, good-bye. She was frying up some hamburger meat while putting away the cheese they used on their children's lunches. Carl was hungry.

Say cheese . . . burger! Kaelin's Restaurant—where cheeseburgers have been on the menu since 1934.

He was about to grab a couple of burgers when he spotted the cheese and had an idea. He said, "Put a little cheese on those hamburgers, Margaret, and let's see what it looks like."

Instant Nirvana.

Kaelin never trademarked the name or even made a big deal of it. But the restaurant's 1934 menu clearly encourages customers, "Try Kaelin's Cheese burgers . . . 15 cents . . . You'll like 'em." Other restaurants have earlier claims on the cheeseburger, but none of them have documentary proof.

Kaelin's Restaurant is at 1801 Newburg Road; (502) 451–1801. Take exit 15, Newburg Road, off I–264 and head north. Then roll down the window and sniff.

THE LOVABLE LUSH

The most famous drunk in history is, of course, a Kentuckian. After all, this is where bourbon originated. Foster Brooks, the comedian known for his "Lovable Lush" character, became famous for staggering onto the set of TV's Dean Martin Show, *slurring his words and coming within an ace of falling down. Martin was always entertained by Brooks's antics and kept him coming back week after week.*

The irony of the Foster Brooks story is that Brooks didn't drink, at least not by the time he became the Lovable Lush. He'd been a bit of a rounder in his younger days, but in 1964 Brooks put down his martini and his cigarette and began leading a sober life.

Brooks grew up in Louisville, where his father was sheriff, his brother was a TV clown, and he was a child singer on the radio. He became a broadcaster, moving to Buffalo, New York, where he anchored radio news and teamed with Bob Schmitt—later Buffalo Bob Smith of The Howdy Doody Show *fame—in a country music band. In 1960, at age forty-eight, he moved his family to Los Angeles to make it as an actor. It took a decade, but an impromptu speech at a celebrity golf tournament led to the creation of his Lovable Lush character. Tournament host Dennis James asked him to tell a few jokes. Brooks decided on the spur of the moment to tell them in his drunk dialect. And thus a legend was born.*

THE BLUEGRASS

THE BLUEGRASS

How will you know when you're in Kentucky's famous Bluegrass region? As soon as the grass turns blue, dummy. Actually that's not true. Bluegrass is not blue. It's—surprise!—green, just like every other kind of grass you've ever seen except dead grass, which is brown.

No, you'll know you're in The Bluegrass when you start passing barns that are nicer than your house. That's because the inhabitants, Thoroughbred racehorses, are worth more than you are. A yearling can go at auction for as much as $4 million. That's a one-year-old horse! The Bluegrass region is responsible for Kentucky's reputation as the home of fast horses and beautiful women. Or is it fast women and beautiful horses?

BEREA SPOONBREAD FESTIVAL
Berea

Spoonbread is not quite corn bread, and actually not quite bread at all. It's, well, spoonbread. Since the early 1990s Berea has held an annual festival celebrating the odd concoction.

Spoonbread was made famous by Boone Tavern at Berea College. It is a mushy, breadlike substance made from corn meal. If you ask the locals to describe it, they'll tell you it's a "corn bread soufflé." (Don't tell them, but it still tastes like mush.)

The festival itself doesn't really celebrate the bread. Instead, it celebrates the fame the bread has brought the region. Drawing crowds of more than 10,000 each year, participants partake in a 5K run, hot air balloon displays, softball tournaments, and the crowning of Miss Berea—all the usual stuff you find in a small town festival, plus spoonbread. The Spoonbread Festival is held the Friday following Labor Day in Memorial Park.

For information call (606) 986–9760.

HOME OF POST-IT NOTES
Cynthiana

There was a time, although it's hard to remember, without Post-it notes. The reason it's hard to remember is that I don't have a Post-it note to remind me!

Post-it notes are those yellow slips of paper with a sticky streak at one end that keep the world organized. Have trouble remembering doctors' appointments? Put a Post-it note on your computer. In fact, put a Post-it note up to help you remember everything in your life.

Post-it notes have only been around since the seventies. They were invented by 3M Company scientist Art Fry. The problem wasn't in making them stick, it was getting people to use them. 3M resorted to giving little yellow pads of Post-its away just to get people hooked. It worked.

And they're not just yellow slabs anymore. You can get Post-it notes in a veritable rainbow of colors and a plethora of shapes, sizes, even scents. To be more precise they come in twenty-seven sizes, fifty-six shapes, fifty-seven colors, and twenty fragrances, including—are you ready for this?—dill pickle.

If you thought you could escape the ubiquitous Post-it note by logging on to your computer, wrong; 3M now has a computer Post-it note. And Cynthiana is Post-it's home; all gazillion of them are manufactured right here.

3M's Post-it manufacturing plant is at 301 New Lair Road. Sorry, there are no tours. 3M doesn't want its secret technology getting into the wrong hands . . . and onto the wrong refrigerators . . . and computer monitors.

BITE THIS BULLET—THE FIRST SUCCESSFUL ABDOMINAL SURGERY
Danville

You've heard the expression "bite the bullet." It usually means get ready for an unpleasant task. But in the olden days, back when Zsa Zsa Gabor was a girl, it literally meant bite the bullet. Someone about to undergo a difficult surgery was given something to bite on to distract the brain from the intense pain. Usually it was a towel or a wooden spoon, but those didn't make for colorful language. So pioneers returning from the Old West would tell tales of biting the bullet, which made for much better copy in dime novels.

Dr. Ephraim McDowell performed the first successful surgical removal of an ovarian tumor in Danville in 1809. And he did it without anesthesia, which didn't bother him but probably wasn't too much fun for his patient. You can see just how primitive this early surgery was—they didn't call physicians "sawbones" for nothing back then—with a visit to Dr. McDowell's office, which has been restored to its early nineteenth-century charm. Well, maybe not charm.

The McDowell House is at 125 South Second Street. Call (859) 236–2804 for information.

THE MOST FAMOUS KENTUCKIAN
(NONATHLETE'S DIVISION)
Frankfort

Without Daniel Boone, where would Kentuckians be? Probably in West Virginia. Born in Berks County, Pennsylvania, on November 2, 1734, to Squire Boone and the former Sarah Morgan, both Quakers, Daniel got a taste of life on the frontier at an early age. That's because his family was kicked out of genteel Berks County when Daniel was fifteen. It seems that his father allowed son Israel to marry a non-Quaker. So the family hit the trail and relocated to Yadkin Valley, North Carolina.

In 1756 Daniel Boone married Rebecca Bryan, but he wasn't home much, which makes you wonder how they managed to have ten kids together. He was always off fighting Indians and conquering land as a frontiersman in what is now Kentucky.

Invasion of the body snatchers. Who's buried in Daniel Boone's grave?
The answer's not as obvious as you might think.

Scholars believe that Boone first saw Kentucky from Pilot Knob in Powell County in 1769. In 1773 Boone failed at his first attempt to settle Kentucky. By 1775, however, he had finally succeeded and had established Boonesborough, a fort about 20 miles southwest of Lexington. But although Boone had finally found success, it was short-lived. Not known for his financial skills, Boone was swindled out of most of his money and the land he had fought for. Embittered, broke, and discouraged, Boone left Kentucky in 1820 to live with his son in Defiance, Missouri, stating that he was leaving because Kentucky "was too crowded."

Things didn't get easier for Boone after he moved. After his death a fight ensued between his family in Missouri and officials in Kentucky for his remains. Kentucky felt that Boone's final resting place should be in Frankfort, where citizens could pay homage to one of their founding fathers. Boone's family, on the other hand, felt that his remains should stay in Missouri because Boone hated Kentucky. Ignoring the family, Kentucky officials traveled to Missouri, dug up the remains, and brought them back to Kentucky.

Or did they?

At the time of Boone's death, he had wished to be buried next to his wife in Missouri. The only problem was that the burial plots next to her were already occupied. So his family buried him at the foot of his wife's grave. Knowing that Kentucky officials were coming to take Boone's remains, they didn't resist. They didn't tell them that they had the wrong body either. Kentucky officials proudly brought back the remains of the body *next* to Rebecca Boone.

In 1983 forensic anthropologists conducted a study on the remains in Frankfort to determine once and for all who had Daniel Boone's body. When the results came back from a plaster cast of the skull, it was determined that the remains in Frankfort belonged to a large black male. Frankfort officials deny the results and insist that they have the true remains of Daniel Boone. If nothing else, they have the largest tombstone.

Boone's bones may or may not be in his grave in Frankfort Cemetery, located at East Main Street.

QUINTESSENTIAL KENTUCKIANS
George Graham Vest

*D*og *has always been man's best friend. It just took a Kentuck-ian to coin the famous phrase.*

Frankfort native George Graham Vest was practicing law in Missouri in 1870 when he took on the case of Charles Burden, whose beloved hunting dog, Old Drum, had been shot by a sheep farmer named Leonidas Hornsby. Burden sued Hornsby in civil court for damages, and Vest gave his famous closing summation, "Tribute to the Dog":

"The best friend a man has in this world may turn against him and become his enemy. His son or daughter that he has reared with loving care may prove ungrateful. Those who are nearest and dear-est to us, those whom we trust with our happiness and our good name, may become traitors to their faith. The money that a man has, he may lose. It flies away from him, perhaps when he needs it most . . . The one absolutely unselfish friend that a man can have in this selfish world, the one that never deserts him and the one that never proves ungrateful or treacherous is his dog . . . Gentlemen of the jury, a man's dog stands by him in prosperity and in poverty, in health and in sickness. He will sleep on the cold ground, where the wintry winds blow and the snow drives fiercely, if only he may be near his master's side. If fortune drives the master forth an outcast in the world, friendless and homeless, the faithful dog asks no higher privilege than that of accompanying him to guard against danger, to fight against his enemies, and when the last scene of all comes and death takes the master in its embrace and his body is laid away in the cold ground, no matter if all other friends pursue their way, there by his graveside will the noble dog be found, his head between his paws, his eyes sad but open in alert watchfulness, faithful and true even to death."

Vest won $50 for his client. When copies of his speech began cir-culating, he won acclaim from dog lovers everywhere and in 1879 was elected to the United States Senate from Missouri. He served four terms.

FRANK LLOYD WRIGHT'S CHEAPEST COMMISSION
Frankfort

Before he was Frank Lloyd Wright, he was Frank Lincoln Wright, his birth name—a budding architect, anxious for any commission that paid cash. Especially anxious to strike out on his own after he left the Chicago architectural firm of Alder and Sullivan, Wright met up with a Frankfort preacher named Jesse Zeigler, who agreed to pay the princely sum— princely for 1900 anyway—of $500 to design his house. That would clock in at about ten grand in today's dollars. Wright gave them one of his "prairie" style designs: a low roof, over-hanging eaves, and lots and lots of glass—enough glass to scandalize many of Zeigler's Presbyterian parishioners. The Zei-glers moved into the house at 509 Shelby Street in 1910, pay-ing $5,000 to the construction company (about $92,000 in today's dollars). The preacher and his family stayed five years before moving on, and the house has passed through many hands since then. It remains one of Wright's cheapest commis-sions (he got 10 percent of the final construction price). In comparison, his commission on Fallingwater was $8,000.

Today the Frank Lloyd Wright home is in immaculate condi-tion thanks to the current owners, Wright fans Jim and Jane Brockman. They have visited more than 300 of his creations. The Brockmans offer half-hour tours, by appointment, for groups of four or more. Admission is $5.00 per person. Call (502) 227-7164 for information and reservations.

HERRY THE HAIRLESS LOCH HERRINGTON MONSTER
Harrodsburg

They say that if you get up early enough and sit on the banks of Lake Herrington long enough, eventually you will see Herry. That's Herry the Lake Monster, Kentucky's answer to Nessie, Scotland's Loch Ness Monster. Herry was first spotted in 1972 by University of Kentucky classics professor Lawrence Thompson. Since then she's reared her ugly head—they say she looks like a catfish with PMS—at fishermen and picnickers. The consensus is that Herry is 15 feet long with a pig snout and a curly tail and God knows what in between. She's seldom spotted after morning, the theory being that she's spooked by the powerboats that take over the lake when powerboaters finally wrest themselves from bed.

What is she, really? Some say she's a giant catfish; others believe she's nothing more than a bobbing bit of driftwood. And a few hold that she really is a monster!

The Lake Herrington Monster has been spotted at Rocky Fork near Dix Dam and in the area between Lake Chenault and Wells Landing. Head to Burgin, just east of Harrodsburg. At the junction of KY 33 and KY 152, take 33 north. A half mile from the junction, when the road veers left, take Curdsville Road straight ahead for 2.5 miles. Turn right at the DIX DOCK sign. This is as close as you can get to Rocky Fork via land. It's off to the left out of sight. Meander over, sit down, and wait.

QUINTESSENTIAL KENTUCKIANS
Adolph Rupp, Baron of The Bluegrass

*T*he Baron of The Bluegrass wasn't born in The Bluegrass. He was born in Halstead, Kansas, and graduated from Kansas University in 1901. But Adolph Rupp is forever linked to Kentucky because he put Kentucky on the map. During his forty-two years as head coach of the University of Kentucky basketball team, 1930 to 1972, he won a then record 876 games, four national championships, and twenty-seven conference championships and made Kentucky a household word during college basketball season.

How did he do it? In a word: desire. Rupp had a competitive streak rivaled by none. He famously said, "I know I have plenty of enemies, but I'd rather be the most hated winning coach in the country than the most popular losing one." Even his players disliked him.

And opposing teams? They were his mortal enemies. During a game in the late forties—a time when Rupp won three national titles—his team held a halftime lead of 38 to 4 over an outmanned team, and still Rupp was raging. It seems that all four of the opponent's points had been scored by a single player. Rupp wanted him stopped. "Somebody guard that man. Why, he's running wild!"

In 1951 Rupp was asked to compare his current team, which would go on to win the NCAA championship, to his '47–'48, which had also won a national title. He responded in typical Rupp fashion. "They [the '48 team] liked to crush everybody early and get it over with. This bunch is tender-hearted—the only one they're killing is me."

Rupp's record of career wins was surpassed in 1997 by University of North Carolina coach Dean Smith, who had the advantage of coaching in an era when teams played more games per season. Had Rupp known that some other coach would surpass his record some day, he most assuredly would have died on the sideline.

LIPS THAT HAVE TOUCHED ALCOHOL OR CIGARETTES SHALL NEVER TOUCH MINE
Lancaster

It must be something in the water. Kentucky, home of bourbon whiskey and burley tobacco, is also home to the most famous temperance crusader and the inventor of the most famous stop-smoking product. That would be Carrie Nation, "the lady with the hatchet," and Frank Etscorn, inventor of the nicotine patch.

Carry "Carrie" Amelia Moore Nation, born in Lancaster, Kentucky, was one of the first crusaders against alcohol. A brief marriage to an alcoholic in the late 1800s was enough to propel Nation to proclaim herself the perpetuator of prohibition. Hers was a quest of the heart, even if she did use force to enforce her beliefs against tobacco and alcohol, Kentucky's chief products. Nation once described herself as "a bulldog running along the feet of Jesus, barking at what he doesn't like."

Nation first "barked" at a bar in Kiowa, Kansas. With her faithful followers, mostly women who had been betrothed to drunks, Nation would barge into local watering holes, encouraging the women to destroy anything that stood in their way. As you can imagine, she wasn't too popular. Most bars would close when they got word that Nation was on her way. They didn't fear her message of prohibition as much as they feared her hatchet. Between 1900 and 1910 Nation was arrested more than thirty times. But her crusade eventually resulted in the passage of the Eighteenth Amendment and more than a decade of Prohibition (which eventually lead to the Twenty-first Amendment: the repeal of Prohibition).

PLEASE, MR. POSTMAN

Next time you mail something via the United States Postal Service, thank Montgomery Blair. Blair, who was Postmaster General under fellow Kentuckian Abraham Lincoln, was born in 1813 in Lexington. He left The Bluegrass for four years to study at West Point but returned in 1835 to get his law degree from Lexington's Transylvania College. He moved to Missouri to practice. It was there that he worked his most famous case: representing slave Dred Scott, whose petition for freedom was denied by the Supreme Court in 1857, paving the way for the Civil War. Even though Blair lost his case, his strong antislavery sympathies brought him to the attention of another Kentucky expatriate, Abraham Lincoln. In gratitude for fighting slavery—and for giving him his convention delegates—Lincoln named him Postmaster General, a big-deal position at the time.

Blair was a clever fellow. In addition to inventing the money order, he established the first military post offices, improved international mail delivery, and abolished franking privileges for local postmasters (franking—free postage—was like a license to print stamps for local postmasters). He was also the only cabinet officer to urge Lincoln to reinforce Fort Sumter in South Carolina, where the first shot of the Civil War was fired. He was a Lincoln loyalist who paid for his loyalty in the end. In 1864 radical Republican John Fremont was gearing up to challenge Lincoln in the presidential race. Fremont agreed to withdraw from the race if Lincoln would sack Blair. Lincoln would—and did.

Blair remained loyal to Lincoln's successor, Andrew Johnson, but when that got him nowhere, he switched to the Democratic Party. His name lives on today with his former Washington residence, the Blair House, now owned by the government and used to house high-ranking foreign dignitaries when they visit this country.

DRIVE-THROUGH MOVIES?
Lexington

Long-haul truck driver Clarence M. Dees was just looking for a little diversion in his life, just a nice carefree afternoon at the movies. So when he got bored with the film he was watching in Theater Four at the North Park Cinemas, he got up and went into Theater Six. That wasn't any better, so he switched back to see the ending of his original movie choice.

During the changeover Dees was spotted and confronted by an officious usher. Words were exchanged and Dees was ejected from the movie house, but he didn't go straight home. Instead he got into the cab of his tractor-trailer and drove it into the theater lobby, ripping out the ceiling, toppling the video games, and nearly demolishing the concession stand. Lexington police officer Fred Williamson (not the action movie star but another Fred Williamson) told the Lexington newspaper, "He wanted to put it in there far enough to see the movie he paid to watch." Charges were filed and Dees was fined.

Remember, don't try this at home.

North Park Cinemas was at 500 New Circle Road Northwest in Lexington. It's now closed. From I–75 take the New Circle Road exit and go south.

I SEE RED! I TASTE PURPLE! SITE OF THE FIRST LSD EXPERIMENTS ON HUMANS
Lexington

Between 1953 and 1962 government doctors tested the psyche-delic drug LSD on 300 human patients, prisoners who were being treated for drug addiction at the U.S. Public Service Hospital in Bracktown. The experiments were funded, just barely, by the CIA. Because there was no money to pay prisoners for their participation, they were given a choice of time off their sentences or the drug of their choice. Most chose drugs. One

Just say no . . . to time off! Drug-addicted prisoners who agreed to take part in government testing of LSD were given a choice of rewards: time off their sentences or the drug of their choice. Most chose the latter.

prisoner told a senate subcommittee that he received morphine for his participation. Pennsylvania Senator Richard Schweicker replied, "I understand now why the percentage of cure at Lexington may not have been too high."

From Lexington take U.S. 421, Leestown Pike, north. The old hospital is on the right, just past Masterson Station Park. It is now the Federal Correction Institute. You can see all you need to from the road.

FRANKLY SCARLETT, I'LL STAY AT BELLE'S
Lexington

She's just about the most famous hooker in history—having taken Rhett Butler in when Scarlett O'Hara tossed him out. The character of Belle Watling was based on Belle Brezing, a Kentucky madam famed for her luxurious brothel, her influential clientele, and the business acumen that gave her a reputation for running "the most orderly of disorderly houses."

Brezing was too young to host soldiers during the Civil War—she was born in Lexington in 1860—but she lived the life for thirty-eight years, from 1879, when she moved into the Jenny Hill brothel, which was housed in the building where Mary Todd Lincoln grew up, till the Army closed her down in 1917.

She opened her own brothel in a rented row house on North Upper Street across from Transylvania University on July 1, 1881. Over the next four decades she variously operated houses at 194 North Upper Street and at 59 Megowan Street. And when she was convicted of running a house of ill repute in 1882, Governor Luke P. Blackburn pardoned her. Hmmmm, interesting that.

Her claim to fame, or infamy, during her career was that she was indicted more times than any other citizen in Lexington. Belle died in 1940. On her cemetery monument is this simple epitaph: BLESSED ARE THE PURE IN HEART.

Belle Brezing is buried in Cavalry Cemetery, Section O, Lot 6. None of her famed "houses" remain. The most notorious was at the corner of Wilson and Megowan. Cavalry Cemetery is at 874 West Main Street. From I–75 take the Paris Road exit (exit 116). It becomes North Broadway, which runs into Main. Turn right on Main.

WILLST THOU LIVETH BEHIND A MOAT
Lexington

First-time cruisers on Lexington's Versailles Road often come to a screeching halt when they round the bend near the airport. They think they've hit a time warp because there on the north side of the highway is a giant castle, complete with stone walls, turrets, drawbridge, and moat. All that's missing is a knight in shining armor—or a band of disgruntled villagers with torches beseeching milord for lower taxes.

There are rumors that the castle was to be a modern-day fairy-tale home for a twentieth-century Lancelot and Guinevere. Or that its owners moved out because it was haunted.

Here's the real story:

Rex and Caroline Martin got the idea for a castle during a European vacation in 1968. They purchased fifty-three acres on U.S. 60 outside Lexington and broke ground in 1969. Their

Be it ever so humble. The couple who built this seven-bedroom, fifteen-bath castle parted ways before it could be finished.

finished estate was to have seven bedrooms, fifteen baths, four corner towers, a dozen turrets, 12-foot-high walls, a draw-bridge, an Italian fountain in the courtyard, and tennis courts in back. But before the castle could be completed, the couple divorced, leaving the place unfinished and empty—and now unsold.

In 1988 the publicity-shy Rex Martin put the castle on the market with a FOR SALE sign that also says APPOINTMENT ONLY and gives a phone number that no one ever answers. At this writing the castle remains unsold, a medieval monument in the middle of horse-farm country that fuels the imagination of all who stop to take a snapshot and even those who merely drive by.

The castle is on Versailles Road, west of Keeneland Race Course, near the Woodford County line.

WHICH ONE OF YOU IS SYBIL?
Lexington

You've seen the 1976 TV movie, the one Sally Fields won an Emmy for her portrayal of multiple personality Sybil Dorsett. The movie was based on the 1973 best-selling book, which, in turn was based on the real life story of Shirley Ardell Mason, who lived quietly in Lexington the last two decades of her life. A few of her Lexington neighbors had their suspicions. After all, Dr. Cornelia Wilbur, a University of Kentucky professor identified in the book as Sybil's psychiatrist, was an almost daily visitor to the Mason house. But most knew Mason as a quiet woman who spent her days dabbing at her watercolor paintings and managing an art and antiques business out of her home.

But *Sybil* was more than just a movie. Before the film was broadcast, "multiple-personality disorder" was considered a rare mental disorder; the American Psychiatric Association didn't even list it in its guidebook as a distinct disease. After the movie there was a boom in reported MPD cases. Thanks, Sybil—and Sybil and Sybil and Sybil and . . .

Mason lived at 345 Henry Clay Boulevard. It is now a private residence.

ONE SMALL STEP FOR WOMAN, ONE GIANT LEAP FOR WOMANKIND
Lexington

Sophonisba Preston Breckinridge—and, yes, that is a mouthful—has a lot of firsts after that name. She was the first woman to receive a Ph.D. in political science; she was the first woman admitted to the Kentucky bar. But her proudest first was the one that was the longest coming: She was the first social worker and single-handedly invented the profession of social work.

Born into a socially prominent Lexington family, Sophonisba graduated from Wellesley College and settled in Washington, D.C., where she taught high school math. But she was restless, and after taking a year off to make the Grand Tour of Europe, she returned to Lexington to study law in her father's law office. She passed the bar, but a year in a law office had convinced her that wasn't her calling either. Then an old college chum invited her to live in Chicago. She jumped at the offer, eventually landing a job in the dean's office at the University of Chicago. With Dean Marion Talbot's help, in 1901 Sophonisba became the first woman to receive a doctoral degree in political science. Restless still, she never pursued a career in politics.

Then in 1906 she began researching employment patterns of women, comparing census data and court records in her quest to determine why some households produced "troubled" kids. The research formed the basis of her book *Back of the Yards,* a study that explored the relationship between public housing and crime and led to her final destination—a career working with the socially disadvantaged, a field she named "social work."

One of her final firsts: creating the School of Civics and Philanthropy at the University of Chicago, a department school that was later renamed the Department of Social Service

Administration. It should be renamed the Sophonisba Preston Breckinridge Department of Social Service Administration. But that may be too much of a mouthful.

PETTICOATS AND SLIDE RULES

All her life Margaret Ingels wanted to be an architect. But when she arrived at the University of Kentucky from her Paris (Kentucky, not France) home in 1910, she discovered that the school had no architectural program. Dean F. Paul Anderson convinced her to try mechanical engineering as "the next best thing." It was a perfect fit. She graduated in 1916 and four years later became the first female to receive the professional degree of Mechanical Engineer.

She worked for the Chicago Telephone Company for a time before joining Carrier Engineering in Pittsburgh, where she began her lifelong love affair with "conditioned air." In 1921 she joined the American Society of Heating and Ventilating Engineers research lab to work on the development of air-conditioning. She became a spokesperson for the mechanical engineering profession, speaking to more than 12,000 people over two decades, delivering a speech she called "Petticoats and Slide Rules."

"The woman who joins the procession of engineers today, tomorrow, and tomorrow's tomorrow benefits by a rich heritage bequeathed to her by those who came before. She assumes automatically the responsibility to further prove that petticoats and slide rules are compatible, and she must not carry the responsibility lightly. Her task is to widen the trails blazed for her—and more. She must build them into great highways for women engineers of the future to travel, free of prejudices and discrimination."

Ingels was inducted into the College of Engineering Hall of Distinction in 1993. As they say in the air-conditioning field: Cool!

THE HORSE WHOSE FUNERAL WAS BROADCAST NATIONALLY ON THE RADIO
Lexington

He was the Muhammad Ali of horse racing. The Greatest. In fact he may even have been more famous than Muhammad Ali. Let's face it: There wasn't all that much else to capture the national attention in the twenties anyway.

His name was Man o' War and he was so famous they even named a road in Lexington after him. What did he do that brought him such fame?

For starters "Big Red," as he was known, won twenty times in twenty-one starts, despite racing only two seasons. He set five world records, even though his handicap was frequently as high as 138 pounds, unheard of today. For comparison's sake, horses in the Kentucky Derby now carry 126 pounds. He won one race, the Lawrence Realization, by 100 lengths. His only loss was in the Sanford Stakes at Saratoga; he was carrying 130 pounds, 15 pounds more than the next closest horse. The big chestnut was backing up when the starter's gun went off, leaving him in the dust. He almost made it up, losing by a mere half length to a horse named Upset. He would go on to beat Upset six times in his career.

When Man o' War died in 1947, he was embalmed and laid out in a custom casket. His funeral was broadcast nationwide on the Mutual Radio Network. Two thousand people attended, and nine people delivered eulogies. He achieved all this fame despite never winning the Kentucky Derby. (He never ran in the most famous of horse races because his trainer thought it too early in the year to run a mile and a quarter.) He was a champion off the track as well, siring 379 offspring, including Triple Crown winner War Admiral and the beloved Seabiscuit.

A bronze statue of Man o' War stands over his grave in the Kentucky Horse Park. The park is located off I–75 at exit 120, 4 miles north of Lexington. Call (800) 678–8813 for information.

MOTHER OF ALL PANCAKES — AUNT JEMIMA'S HOME
Montgomery County

Most states would be proud to have one famous packaged cooking mix call the place home. Kentucky can be doubly proud: We are home to two famous mix masters. Duncan Hines, the guy who lent his name to cake mix, is from Bowling Green (see The Pennyrile chapter). And Nancy Green, better known as Aunt Jemima of pancake mix fame, is from Mount Sterling. Of course neither actually invented the mix that bears his or her name. But that's another story.

Green, a former slave whose face was on pancake mix boxes all over America and became advertising's first living trademark, was born in 1834 in Montgomery County. Green was a renowned cook, but she didn't invent her namesake pancake mix. That credit goes to a couple of white men, Chris L. Rutt and Charles G. Underwood, who bought the Pearl Milling Company of St. Joseph, Missouri, in the 1880s. They weren't planning on being millers. They had bigger ideas; they wanted a product. Packaged food was becoming all the rage—witness the popularity of prepackaged cereal by the Kellogg Brothers of Battle Creek, Michigan—and they hit upon the idea of a ready-mixed, self-rising pancake flour. The name for their product came from a chance evening Rutt spent at a minstrel show where he saw a performer in apron and bandana sing a catchy tune named "Aunt Jemima." As he exited the theater everyone was humming the song, and he knew he had a name for his pancake mix. While Rutt and Underwood were long on imagination, they were short on cash and went broke—but not before selling their pancake product to the R. T. Davis Milling Company in 1890.

Davis decided that he needed a spokeswoman. He found Nancy Green in Chicago, where she was the housekeeper for a judge and where the World's Columbian Exposition was being held in 1893. There Davis put her in front of the world's largest flour barrel and instructed her to play the part of Aunt Jemima. She did, charming the crowd so much that fair officials had to hire extra policemen to keep the throngs moving in front of the booth. Davis put Green on the road, and she spent the next thirty years, until her death in 1923 at age eighty-nine, promoting pancakes. Her image lives on today on the pancake mix box that bears her "adopted" name, Aunt Jemima. Yes, it's been updated so that Aunt Jemima has lost the bandana, but look closely and you can still see Nancy Green's smile.

Court Day
Mount Sterling

What brings over 100,000 people to eastern Kentucky for three days in October? Guns. But it's not hunting season. It's trading season, and the occasion is the largest swap meet in the state: Court Day.

Every year, the third Monday in October is declared Court Day in Mount Sterling, Kentucky. But since this is Kentucky, Court Day is more than just one day: It's also the Saturday and Sunday preceding the third Monday of October.

Court Day began at the turn of the nineteenth century when the General Assembly passed a law stating that each county should meet at least once a month to handle all court and business affairs. Due to its location between neighboring counties, Mount Sterling became a trading-post mecca. People from all over gathered for three days to trade mules, turkeys, geese, trapped wild animals, sorghum molasses, vegetables, ponies, horses, and, of course, guns. Hey, our founding father is Daniel Boone after all.

Gone are the mules, horses, and other livestock, but you can still find plenty of fresh produce, crafts, and country goods. The biggest draw to the festival now is guns. If you ask the right people, though, you could probably still find a mule. There's a reason Mount Sterling's motto is "Where the bluegrass meets the mountains."

For more information on Court Day, call (859) 498–8732.

*S*ee *M*c*G*uffey *W*rite
Paris

In 1823 Pennsylvania native William Holmes McGuffey was just a pup, a mere twenty-three, when he hired on at the Paris subscription school, located in a converted smokehouse. McGuffey wrote to his brother that he was assembling his reading book because so few of the students in his classroom could read. He remained for four years, putting his off-hours to good use as he assembled a collage of poems, essays, short stories, and speeches for his Reader.

First published in 1836 the Readers—the first was known as the *Peerless Pioneer Reader*—were wildly popular, eventually selling more than 120 million copies. They have a reputation for being stern, but in fact McGuffey drew on all manner of literature, from Dickens to Longfellow, to make his books fun to read. The McGuffey Readers became one of the most widely read series of books of nineteenth-century America and among the most influential.

The school/smokehouse is gone. It was located on High Street on the south side of Public Square in downtown Paris. There's a historical marker to guide you to the site.

Stop! Birthplace of the Man Who Invented the Traffic Light
Paris

If Garrett Morgan had never lived, what a mess traffic would be in! It was Morgan who invented the traffic light, a mechanism that made it safe for motorists to approach an intersection.

Morgan, who was born on a farm in Paris to two former slaves, was always a tinkerer. So when he moved to Cleveland, Ohio, in 1895 he had no trouble landing a job as a repairman at a sewing machine manufacturer. Because he was so good he soon had his own repair company. While driving to work one day, he witnessed as a car and a horse-drawn carriage both charged into an intersection. The collision gave him an idea. He sketched it the design for a T-shaped pole with three signs on it: STOP, GO, and a third sign that stopped traffic in all directions so that pedestrians could cross. He patented his invention in 1923, and soon Morgan Traffic Signals were all over the country. GE,

Thomas Edison's company, was so impressed that it bought Morgan's patent for $40,000. Morgan sold out just in time, because the tricolored traffic light soon supplanted his invention.

Morgan never stopped experimenting and later invented a zigzag stitching attachment for sewing machines and a gas mask. He attracted national attention when he donned the mask and rescued several men trapped by an explosion in an underground tunnel beneath Lake Erie. The Morgan gas mask was later adopted by the U.S. Army during World War I and by fire departments all across the country.

FLOAT LIKE A PAIR OF BUTTERFLIES: THE TWO CASSIUS CLAYS
Richmond

Although they were born more than a century apart, people continue to confuse Kentucky's two Cassius Clays. In fact, a few years ago Lexington's WKYT television station produced a documentary on White Hall, the historic home of famed nineteenth-century abolitionist Cassius Clay. When the program was listed in *TV Guide,* an editor spotted what he thought was an error and changed the show's synopsis to note that White Hall was the former home of Muhammad Ali.

That's the problem we have in Kentucky: two, two, two famous Cassius Clays. The first Cassius Marcellus Clay, born 1810, was a man of many accomplishments: He was a newspaper publisher, a naturalist, a founder of the national Republican Party, and an orator—an occupation that no longer exists (modern equivalent of an orator: a motivational speaker minus the tapes, books, and infomercials). From 1861 to 1869 he was U.S. minister to Russia. He is even credited with convincing

President Abraham Lincoln to sign the Emancipation Proclamation. Like a true Kentuckian, at age eighty-four this first Cassius Clay married a fifteen-year-old girl.

The second Cassius Marcellus Clay, born in Louisville in 1942, was a boxer—but not just any boxer. He was the self-proclaimed Greatest, and he may just have been. For certain he was the most colorful boxer of all time, given to such pronouncements as "Boxing's just a job. Grass grows, birds fly, waves pound the sand. I just beat people up." He also was a man of many accomplishments—Olympic champion, three-time heavyweight champion—and an orator in his own right.

His boxing philosophy: "The fight is won or lost far away from witnesses—behind the lines, in the gym, and out there on the road, long before I dance under those lights." His life philosophy: "Prejudice comes from being in the dark; sunlight disinfects it."

In 1964 Clay the boxer changed his name to Muhammad Ali to reflect his embrace of the Muslim faith. Numerous sources claim that he is the most famous living person in the world.

White Hall is located at 500 White Hall Shrine Road in Richmond. Take exit 95 east from I-75. Call (859) 623-9178 for information.

ERNEST P. REDNECK, ESQUIRE DELUXE

*I*f you have children, or if you are children, then you know
Ernest. That's Ernest P. Worrell, Esquire Deluxe, for those
who don't. Ernest is the annoying but good-hearted soul who
saves the world and Santa and the kids in the neighborhood
in a string of Ernest comedies that came from Disney Studios
in the eighties and nineties.

The Ernest character was created out of whole cloth by
Lexington native, the late Jim Varney. Varney sort of practiced for the Ernest part as a semiregular on the late seventies TV series America 2-Night, a spin-off of Mary Hartman,
Mary Hartman. He played the recurring character of mobile
home daredevil Virgil Sims, an early incarnation of Ernest P.
if there ever was one. The long-faced Virgil would appear on
the talk show spoof periodically to boast of his recent
exploits: He would jump his mobile home over an increasing
number of cars.

When he was hired for a commercial touting Beech Bend
Park in western Kentucky, he created Ernest P. The park
went under, but Varney's career went straight up. There were
nine Ernest comedies in all, each one more outrageous than
the next.

In a 1984 interview Varney told the author how he found
the Ernest P. in himself. He confided that he grew up around
quite a few Ernest P. Worrell's in Kentucky. "They kind of
flourish in this part of the country." Varney died on February
10, 2000.

THE MOUNTAINS

THE MOUNTAINS

When people outside Kentucky think of Kentuckians, many think of a tobacco-chewing, toothless illiterate with raggedy clothes, a flintlock musket, and a whiskey still behind the tumbledown cabin—a hillbilly, in other words. That's the image they've seen on TV and in comic strips ("Snuffy Smith") over the years. Okay, there are people in the mountains who have poor dental hygiene, no reading skills and a strong love of illegal drink. But that doesn't begin to touch the diversity of the population.

TV, in particular satellite TV, has brought the outside world to the hollers and hilltops of the Appalachian Mountains (and if you hear people pronounce it *ap-uh-LAY-chuns* instead of *ap-uh-LATCH-uns,* be assured they aren't from around here). Mountain folk aren't isolated anymore.

In the mountains we now have mansions and luxury cars and satellite dishes. In fact the owner of the largest private collection of Rolls Royce cars is or was a Kentucky mountaineer. (Maybe you saw the story on *60 Minutes.* He was a coal mine owner back in the heyday of coal mining.) There aren't many illegal stills left. The major illicit export is no longer moonshine; it's marijuana.

The modern world has arrived in the mountains. In fact it got here several decades ago; it just took the media a while to figure that out. Now some of the most respected writers and artists and businesspeople in the world are from our mountains.

KYLE CAMPBELL, 1999 WORLD AMATEUR POLE BENDING CHAMPION
Corbin

Knox County is the home of Kyle Campbell, 1999 World Amateur Pole Bending Champion. At least that's what the sign out on the bypass proclaims. Lest you think it's a joke, let me take this opportunity to set you straight. Kyle Campbell is, or was, the 1999 World Amateur Pole Bending Champion. But

Looks great on a resume! Just one question: How many people does one have to beat to become the amateur pole bending champion?

pole bending is not what you think. It doesn't involve muscle men hanging around a motel ballroom, taking turns bending ever-stiffer metal poles. Pole bending is an equestrian event. That's right: horses are involved.

Its closest relative is barrel racing, which you've probably seen on Sunday-morning TV. But instead of racing horses around barrels, competitors race their mounts around poles, six of them in all, that are 6 feet high and positioned 21 feet apart.

It's a very difficult event. Your horse must change leads (lead foot) while making this serpentine run through pole after pole. Not just anyone can excel at pole bending. But Kyle Campbell can and did in 1999, when he won the World Amateur event.

Salute him as you drive past his roadside monument on U.S. 25 just east of Corbin.

COLONEL SANDERS ORIGINAL RESTAURANT
Corbin

K entucky has many stories of men and their chickens. Most of those stories, however, are not fit to print. One man, though, stands apart from the others—a man with a vision, a man who achieved worldwide fame and success. That chicken loving man was Colonel Harland Sanders.

Sanders, or "the Colonel" as he is better known, didn't begin his chicken career until he was forty. The Colonel owned a service station in Corbin, where he got the bright idea that he could make a little extra money if he could somehow combine his service station with a restaurant.

What came first, the chicken or the egg?
If you're in Kentucky, it's definitely the chicken.

With his mission in mind, the Colonel opened his restaurant within the service station, using his own dining room table. He could seat only six, but it was six more than he had before. As he served his home-cooked meals, the Colonel's reputation grew. Soon he was able to open the Sanders Cafe in 1937, which seated 142 customers. The Colonel was moving up!

All the while he was working the service station and cafe, the Colonel was also working to perfect his "secret" recipe of eleven herbs and spices. He also experimented with ways to cook the chicken faster, designing a pressure cooker.

In 1960 the Colonel franchised the Kentucky Fried Chicken (KFC) restaurant chain and had more than 600 restaurants by 1964. The Colonel's popularity and image grew fast. By 1976 the Colonel's mug was so popular that he was voted the second most recognizable celebrity in the world.

The Colonel died on December 16, 1980. The man most people identified with the state of Kentucky through his KFC restaurants was given a state funeral, complete with visitation in the state capitol in Frankfort. He was buried in Cave Hill Cemetery, Louisville.

It should be noted that old-timers in Corbin will tell you that locally the Colonel wasn't famous for his fried chicken but for his country ham.

A Kentucky Fried Chicken restaurant is located inside Sanders Cafe, on U.S. 25 West. The only admission is a healthy appetite. Call (606) 528–2163 for current restaurant hours. There's also a Colonel Sanders museum at KFC headquarters in Louisville, 1441 Gardiner Lane; (402) 456–8353.

COLONEL SANDERS BY THE NUMBERS

6:	Seats in Harland Sanders's first restaurant—his own dining room table in the living quarters of his Corbin service station
11:	Herbs and spices in the Colonel's secret recipe for fried chicken
40:	The Colonel's age when he started developing his secret recipe
65:	The Colonel's age when he began franchising his chicken recipe
600:	Kentucky Fried Chicken franchises in 1964
2,000,000:	Dollars John Y. Brown and Jack Massey paid Sanders for his business in 1964
5,231:	Kentucky Fried Chicken (now KFC) restaurants in 2002
2 billion:	KFC dinners served annually
9:	Pieces of KFC Chicken consumed annually by every man, woman, and child in the USA
2:	Rank of Col. Sanders in 1976 among world's most recognizable faces

NIAGARA OF THE SOUTH AND GRAND CANYON OF THE SOUTH

Cumberland Falls and Cumberland Gap

*A*nd both are located right here in Kentucky! There are two Niagara Falls—one in the North in New York/Ontario and one in the South in Kentucky. But ours is better.

Located in Daniel Boone National Forest, Cumberland Falls plunges more than 125 feet to a rock-lined bed. The falls are also more than 60 feet wide. This all sounds like pretty standard falls stuff, not much different from Niagara. Here's why Cumberland Falls is better: Kentucky's Cumberland Falls are home to the only moonbow in the Western Hemisphere. The moonbow is a natural phenomenon of a beam of light, from the moon of course, that shoots across the falls. It is visible in the mist of the falls and can be viewed only on a clear night lit by a full moon.

Take that Niagara!

While Cumberland Falls is considered the Niagara of the South, Cumberland Gap is the Grand Canyon of the South—the only break in the Cumberland Mountains and a famous exploring path.

The first records of the Gap are from surveyor Dr. Thomas Walker in 1750. Walker's fame came not from exploring the Gap but from his relationship to Thomas Jefferson. Walker was the doctor for Jefferson's father, Peter. When Peter died, Walker was entrusted as young Jefferson's guardian. After being bitten by the surveying and exploring bug, Walker left medicine behind and plunged ahead to the Gap. His journal entries of what he saw on April 13, 1750, are the first recordings that are known of the Cumberland Gap.

Of course, Walker wasn't the first person to find the Gap. Archeologists believe that animals used the Gap in prehistoric times for migratory purposes. Native Americans, too, are thought to have taken advantage of the Gap's geographical location. The Gap borders three states that were known for their natural bounty: Tennessee, Virginia, and Kentucky.

Due to its location, the Gap served as a coveted position during the Civil War, and over the course of the war, it exchanged hands more than ten times. In 1861 the Confederates seized the Gap, only to abandon it in 1862. After that, General George W. Morgan of the Union took control. The Confederates returned and kicked the Union soldiers out. On September 7, 1863, Major General Ambrose Burnside of the Union took control yet again of the Gap for a final time. In 1864 Ulysses S. Grant declared the Gap the "Gibraltar of America!"

In June 1940 Cumberland Gap became the largest historical park in the country, with more than 20,000 acres of land.

Cumberland Falls State Resort Park is located at 7351 Highway 90 in Corbin. For information call (606) 528-4121. For information about Cumberland Gap National Historical Park call (606) 248-2817.

Niagara Falls has nothing on Cumberland Falls.

FROGTOWN: BIRTHPLACE OF THE "SHORTEST" PRESIDENT

You probably didn't read about him in history class. That's because he's conveniently missing from most history texts. But the shortest U.S. president—in length of service, that is—David Rice Atchison, was from Frogtown.

Atchison, President Pro Temp of the Senate, served a mere twenty-four hours when James K. Polk's term expired and the very religious Zachary Taylor refused to take office on a Sunday. It happened on March 4, 1849. Polk left office at midnight. Taylor refused to take office on March 4 because it was a Sunday, so Atchison was president for a day—the most uneventful presidency in U.S. history.

Atchison himself didn't consider it a major achievement. In fact when asked what he did during his one day as the nation's chief executive, he told a reporter that he slept through most of it. "I went to bed. There had been two or three busy nights finishing up the work of the Senate, and I slept most of that Sunday." His hometown of Frogtown has since been renamed Kirklevington for obvious reasons. Who would want a president from Frogtown?

POKE SALLET FESTIVAL
Harlan

Thanks to Tony Joe White, at least a few people have heard of poke sallet. They think it's a salad and that it was invented by Annie—thus his 1969 hit record "Poke Salad Annie"—but at least they are in the ballpark.

Actually it's a weed, not "the" weed, but a weed nonetheless, and every spring the folks of Harlan celebrate it with the Poke Sallet Festival.

Poke sallet has been a food staple for mountain people since the Depression. Food was scarce and money to buy it was even harder to come by. Then someone stumbled upon this weed that grew in abundance in abandoned coal mines. It looks like a green, and some say it tastes similar to a green, so they ate it. Thus began the culinary history of the poke sallet. In tribute, every year the festival has a poke sallet cooking contest, where chefs compete for best recipe.

Most natives and regular poke sallet eaters agree that the best way to cook it is to fry it in bacon grease. However, before you grab a fork and dig in, be forewarned: Poke sallet is poisonous. It has become a hot topic in the science community. Some scientists believe that it may hold the key to treating AIDS and arthritis. Others believe that poke sallet causes cancer, intestinal disease, and birth defects. The only thing any of the scientists agree on is that the root and berry of poke sallet is poisonous. Most mountain people don't believe this, though, and state that if it hasn't killed them yet, there's no harm.

For more information call (606) 573–4717.

MULLET HEAD

*I*t's the haircut of a thousand names: the Tennessee Tophat (because of its popularity among country music fans), the Mississippi Mudflap (because that's what it looks like), the Ape Drape, the Soccer Rocker, and Hockey Hair. It's even been called the Kentucky Waterfall (for the precipitous drop the locks make). Hairdressers call it the Bi-Level. Barbers call it by its most common appellation, the Mullet. It's the male haircut that's short in front and long in back. And it's most famous devotee is Flatwoods, Kentucky, native Billy Ray Cyrus, the country music star famous for his hit records "Some Gave All," "Trail of Tears," and "Achy Breaky Heart." That last hit has given the Mullet yet another name. People who don't like the haircut have been known to call it the Achy-Breaky-Mistake-y!

JOHN SWIFT'S KENTUCKY MOTHER LODE
Johnson County (or Is It Martin County?)

John Swift was a sailor and an adventurer who on his death-bed in Virginia in the late 1700s told a tale of incalculable wealth. Swift related how he and his friend, George Munday, were partners in a Kentucky silver mine, the Kentucky Mother Lode. Oh, and what a lode it was; the vein was 3 feet high. Swift and Munday had had a falling out, and he had killed Munday then turned to smelting all the silver for himself. He worked for fifteen months, then crated the silver up and hid it in a cave in the Appalachian Mountains of eastern Kentucky.

He made his way back to his hometown of Alexandria, Virginia, seeking help in retrieving his fortune. But no one believed him. He was just another crazy old man, they said, and Swift died blind and penniless.

But not everyone doubted his tale. Over the years hundreds of fortune hunters have made their way to the mountains, searching for this cave located in the shadow of a "peculiar looking rock"—a stone supposedly shaped like a turtle with markings resembling turkey tracks on top.

No one has ever found it.

That's one version of the story. Others have the mine or mines in Virginia or Tennessee or North Carolina. But all agree on one thing: There's a fabulous load of silver somewhere in a mountain cave, just waiting to be found.

WORLD CHICKEN FESTIVAL
London

When it comes to chicken, the folks of Laurel County do chicken right. And well they should, since the place was home to Colonel Harland Sanders's first restaurant and also the first restaurant of Lee Cummings, Colonel Sanders's nephew and the cofounder of Lee's Famous Recipe Chicken.

So each September they drag out the World's Largest Stainless Steel Skillet, fry up a mess of chicken, and pay tribute to

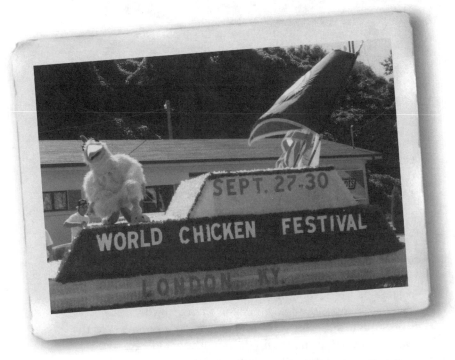

*Kids and grownups alike are promised an eggs-cellent time
at the World Chicken Festival.*

Will the real Colonel Sanders please stand up?

this heritage with their annual eggs-travaganza, the World Chicken Festival. The skillet is 10.5 feet in diameter and 8 inches deep with an 8-foot handle. It would not work for a pancake festival because it weighs 700 pounds and would require several Arnold Schwarzneggers to flip. The skillet holds 300 gallons of cooking oil and can cook 600 quarters of chicken at a time.

A quarter million people are "eggs-pected" each fall for the four-day event. They are filled with "eggs-citement"—and also with chicken. More than 30,000 fried chicken dinners have been fried up in the giant skillet since its creation in 1992. They serve up more fried chicken than anywhere else in the world during the festival—and also make more uses of the word "eggs" in puns than you thought could eggs-ist.

For information call (800) 348–0095.

JAILBIRD JUDGE
Louisa

In addition to being the birthplace of the Hanging Judge, Judge Roy Bean (born in Mason County in 1825), Kentucky is also the home state of Frederick Vinson, the only Chief Justice of the United States Supreme Court born in jail.

That's right: the only Chief Justice of the United States Supreme Court born in jail—not that any other Chief Justices have clamored to argue the distinction. But Vinson was proud of the fact and amused the Washington cocktail set with his boast.

How did it happen? When Vinson was born in 1890, his father was the jailer in Louisa. The family lived in an apartment in the jail and that's where Vinson was born.

Fred also holds the distinction of never missing a Centre College football game—even though he has been dead since 1953. Brothers of his old fraternity, Phi Delta Theta, adopted the habit of taking his portrait—affectionately dubbed Dead Fred—to home football and basketball games, and he's been in attendance at every game for the last four decades. In fact he was in the audience of the vice-presidential debate held at Centre in 2000.

LITTLE BANG THEORY
Middlesboro

It was long before CNN and Fox News, so there wasn't much coverage. In fact there was *no* coverage when a giant meteor a quarter mile in diameter crashed down in southeastern Kentucky 300 million years ago, creating a crater some 4 miles wide. Daniel Boone was several million years from crossing into Kentucky through the Cumberland Gap. But jump ahead to, oh, 1889, and watch as the Middlesborough Town Company, an English corporation, buys land in the Cumberland Gap area and founds the town of Middlesborough, better known today as Middlesboro.

The site they picked for their city was in the heart of the meteor crater, though they didn't know it. But their astute judgment makes Middlesboro the only city in the United States built in a meteor crater.

FIRST COMMERCIAL OIL WELL

The nation's first commercial oil well was a mistake. Located in McCreary County, the well was originally drilled in search of brine used by salt makers. However, once drilling began in 1818, they found that they had struck gold. The well, known as the Martin Beatty Well, produced large quantities of oil. Kentucky's production of oil didn't stop there. The people of Exxon got involved and have the record of the deepest oil well, at a depth of more than 15,000 feet. Henderson County holds the state's record of the most oil produced, at 109 million barrels.

PREPARED TO MEET GOD
Middlesboro

arrison Mayes had a vision. While pinned against the wall of a Kentucky coal mine by a runaway coal car, the life being squeezed from him, he saw a cross. But not just any cross—a giant cross. "I said, Lord if you'll let me live, I'll build it," Mayes told me in 1980, seven years before his death.

And he did—a large cross of light bulbs on the mountain overlooking Middlesboro's east side. But he didn't stop there. He built a concrete mold and began pouring cement crosses, hundreds of them, which he transported all over the country, erecting these roadside religious monuments warning JESUS IS COMING SOON and PREPARE TO MEET GOD all over the southern United States. If you drove to Florida on vacation in the years before interstates, you probably saw one of his crosses.

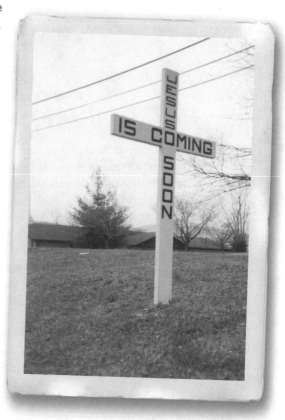

Cross my heart and hope not to die. Harrison Mayes promised "Lord, if you let me live, I'll build it." And he did.

But he didn't stop there, either. He built a new home in the shape of a cross. Mayes told me he once had a cross-shaped sign out front of his house that read IF YOU GO TO HELL IT'S YOUR OWN FAULT. The neighbors complained so much that he finally took it down.

Many of the crosses have crumbled or been bulldozed for highway expansion. But his cross-shaped house remains, a monument to one man's obsession with a religious symbol. It's at 409 Chester Avenue, which runs off the main drag in downtown, KY 74 West. The home is still a private residence.

OLDEST CONTINUOUSLY PLAYED U.S. GOLF COURSE
Middlesboro

Want to see how golf was played a hundred years ago without having to charter a flight to Scotland? Then visit the Middlesboro Country Club, which claims to be "the oldest continuously played golf course in the United States."

The golf club was founded in 1889 by a group of English investors who had immigrated to the Cumberland Gap region. They founded the town, laying out wide English-style streets and building Tudor homes. But they sorely missed their beloved game of golf. After scouting the area a bit, they discovered the Yellow Creek Valley and deemed it a suitable place for the building of a golf course.

Middlesboro Country Club retains its original layout, and that includes the 200-year-old oaks that were lining the fairways when the club was built more than a century ago. It's only a nine-hole course, but in 1889 that was quite an undertaking to build.

There are older golf clubs in the country. The Country Club of Charleston (South Carolina), for instance, was founded in

1786. But all the others closed for long periods of time. There is no older club where golf has been played continuously.

Middlesboro Country Club is a private club, but it welcomes visitors. For information call (606) 248–3831.

THE HUNDRED MILLION DOLLAR HOLE
Middlesboro

I t's an impressive hole, drilled straight through Cumberland Mountain. But it's still just a hole.

The hole has a name—the Cumberland Gap Tunnel—and there is no question that it is a marvel of modern engineering technology. It cost $280 million and took seventeen years to burrow the 1-mile hole through the hill. The nickname the Hundred Million Dollar Hole comes from the early years of the project. That was the initial projection of how much it would cost. Someone forgot to figure in cost overruns.

The Cumberland Gap Tunnel opened in 1996 and carries U.S. Highway 25–E from Kentucky to Tennessee and Virginia. It replaced a road that followed the old Wilderness Trail through Cumberland Gap, meaning that old road that meandered up the hill taking the same course a cow would. As one of the most deadly stretches of highway in the country, it had to be replaced. An average of one death occurred there every month, and locals called it "Massacre Mountain."

The tunnel did the deed. There hasn't been a fatality along this stretch of road since it opened, even though traffic on the highway has doubled. The local congressman, Hal Rogers, calls it "the most significant thing that has happened here since Daniel Boone began to bring settlers through the Gap." He's right.

The Cumberland Gap Tunnel is on U.S. 25–E between Middlesboro and Cumberland Gap.

THE STRANGE MUSIC FESTIVAL
Olive Hill

No it's not a festival devoted to Yoko Ono music. It's a celebration of those industrious and inventive Kentucky mountain people who over the years have managed to make music from the most unusual items. An instrument qualifies as "strange" as long as it was not intended to be musical.

Can't afford a drum set? You can make music by strumming on a washboard. Over the years participants have played everything from bedpans to body parts, drinking glasses, and eyeglasses. John Tierney, the festival founder, always brings the crowd to its feet playing his tongue. Yes, it can be done. It's a cluck, cluck, clicking sound, but it's definitely a tune. Tierney, now retired from his post as park naturalist, came up with the idea in the seventies as a way to draw attention to this off-the-beaten-path state resort park.

For information call (606) 286–4411.

HOMEGROWN HUSTLER

Scratch the surface of First Amendment champion Larry Flynt and you'll find a hustler at heart. That's how he grew up in the backwoods of northern Kentucky—and that's how he made his name: hustling a lowbrow porn magazine named Hustler.

Flynt grew up dirt poor in dirt poor Magoffin County. "The biggest industry was jury duty," he once told the Louisville Courier-Journal.

In 1958 the sixteen-year-old Flynt used his 1951 Ford to run bootleg whiskey around the county. He made his name in the skin trade after moving to Dayton, Ohio, and opening a strip club in 1965. The first Hustler Club opened there in 1968. The magazine named for the club debuted in 1974 to underwhelming reviews (another magazine called it the most boring publication in America except for Refrigerator Monthly).

The magazine was headed for oblivion until Flynt bought nude photos of Jacqueline Kennedy Onassis from a spy photographer in 1975 for $18,000. And thus the modern Hustler was born.

IT'S RAINING . . . MEAT?

*I*t was a clear, cloudless March day in 1876. Home-maker Mrs. Allan Crouch was in the yard of her Bath County farm making soap when she felt something smack her on the head. She rubbed the smarting spot and found blood—but not her own. It was blood from the falling object. She was pummeled by falling meat, what would later be called the Famous Meat Shower. It was thin-sliced, and when it was all over, what amounted to a horse wagon full of the stuff had fallen on her yard.

There were no tornadoes or storms of any kind in the area that could have carried the meat to her home in the shadow of Carrington Rock. It was a good quarter century before the Wright Brothers, so the stuff couldn't have been dumped by an aircraft. The Famous Meat Shower was investigated by a team of professors from Transylvania College in Lexington, but no explanation was ever found.

Carrington Rock is 3 miles south of Olympia Springs on KY 36.

BIG, SCARY AND SQUARE

It was a hot July night in 1986 and Mary Helton was finishing up at her Countryside Restaurant in Oneida. Suddenly a large object loomed in the sky over Bullskin Mountain. "It was very big, scary, and square with windows," she would later tell the Manchester Enterprise. *If Helton were the only one to observe the big, scary, and square UFO, it would be easy to discount. But scores of other people in the area called the newspaper, the airport, and the weather station.*

Air traffic controllers at the London airport insisted it must have been a B-52 flying low overhead, but locals insisted that they had seen airplanes—and this was no airplane. It was flying too low and too slow.

The newspaper investigated, but no explanation was ever found. The good news is that the big, scary, square object has never returned.

HOME OF THE FEUDING McCOYS
Pikeville

Let's take a trip down to Pike County, Kentucky, to play a game of family feud.

The feud between the West Virginia Hatfields and the Kentucky McCoys is perhaps the longest and best-known family rivalry. The rivalry has outlasted the original family descendents, been intertwined through marriages, and claimed the lives of thirteen persons and one pig. In fact, a pig is what started the whole ordeal.

The Hatfields and McCoys were very much patriarchal families and run by the men of the house, which was the custom of the time and the mountain region. Randolph "Ole Ran'l" McCoy was not known for his charm. He was often described by members of his own clan as "mean" and "grumpy." Ole Ran'l and his wife, Sarah, who also happened to be his cousin, had a total of fifteen children—nine boys and six girls.

Captain William Anderson "Devil Anse" Hatfield was the mirror image of Ole Ran'l. Devil Anse was known for his charm, wit, and, most of all, his humor. With his wife, Levicy, Devil Anse had thirteen children—nine boys and four girls.

A game of sorts developed between the two families, members of whom snuck over the border to steal each other's pigs and horses. This game of thievery never amounted to more than a slight inconvenience for both families.

While the game of "they stole my pig" never really made waves, Ole Ran'l had had enough by the fall of 1878. Ole Ran'l had gone to visit a Kentucky Hatfield who had married his sister when he spotted a pig that looked familiar to him (no one quite knows exactly how Ole Ran'l "knew'" the pig so to speak, but he did). Ole Ran'l told his brother-in-law Floyd that the pig was his and accused him of stealing from kin, a grave sin. Floyd denied all accusations of theft and said that the pig had always been his. Ole Ran'l took Floyd to court to settle the matter once and for all.

Anse Hatfield served as judge over the case, and the jury consisted of six McCoys and six Hatfields. The entire case hinged on the testimony of Bill Staton, who swore that Floyd rightfully owned the pig. Staton just happened to be the brother-in-law of Ellison Hatfield, who was Devil Anse's brother. Floyd won the case.

Ole Ran'l was furious at the outcome, so much so that he put a hit out on both Staton and the pig. Shortly after the trial, Staton was shot by Paris and Sam McCoy. Sam stood trial for the murder but was acquitted because Devil Anse got involved and persuaded the jury to find him not guilty as a sign of truce between the two families. The gesture was lost on Ole Ran'l, who felt that Sam should not have had to go to trial in the first place. War between the two clans was declared. The feud and killing went back and forth until it finally came to an end in 1891. The final death toll was thirteen—plus the pig.

Both patriarchs lived long lives, well into their 80s. Ole Ran'l died March 28, 1941. Devil Anse became a born again Christian and died January 6, 1921, from pneumonia. Ole Ran'l McCoy is buried in the Dils Cemetery at U.S. 460 and Old U.S. 23 Bypass. For information call (800) 844-7453.

"P"
IS FOR
PEPSI—AND
FOR PIKEVILLE

There are some curiosities for which there is no explanation. This is one of them. Pikeville annually leads the nation in per capita consumption of Pepsi Cola. It's not a recent phenomenon. It's a long-standing love affair by a town for a drink. Pepsi wasn't invented here (it was created in North Carolina), and there's no known connection. People in Pikeville just prefer Pepsi. (Try saying that five times real fast.)

Even a 2001 commemorative Coke bottle celebrating the town's Hillbilly Days Festival didn't change the equation. Coke sold out of the bottle with the hillbilly on it, but Pepsi remained number one in local supermarkets.

HILLBILLY FESTIVAL
Pikeville

Pikeville, the county seat of Pike County, Kentucky, is home to the most notable hillbillies of all time, the McCoys. It's also home to the Hillbilly Days Festival.

Organized by Howard "Dirty Ear" Stratton and "Shady" Grady Kinney, the festival began in 1977 as an effort to raise money for the Shriner's Children's Hospitals and Burn Centers. Mountain clans from all over the nation turned out for the "family reunion."

Downtown Pikeville is transformed into an outdoor festival complete with dance floor for the clogging and square dance competitions. Mountain music permeates the area, and children and adults of all ages participate in the hillbilly costume contest.

Hillbilly Days are held every April. For festival information call (800) 844–7453.

NATURAL BRIDGE
Slade

It's a rock that goes from one hill to another. Yep, a rock.

The natural bridge measures 78 feet long and 65 feet high—yet most people never know they're on it.

To get to the bridge you can take a lift or torture yourself with stair climbing. Once you get to the top there are no markers, no large arrows pointing to it, no sign that says YOU'RE ON

IT. When most people get to the bridge, they are impressed with the scenery and large drop-off on both sides. But they rarely recognize that they wouldn't be able to see the beauty around them if they weren't standing on, say it with me, a bridge. The bridge cloaks itself in the surrounding area, hence the term "natural."

So when you go to see the natural bridge and find yourself standing high in the hills, taking in the bountiful scenery and wondering where this bridge that you've come so far to see is, look down. You're on it.

Natural Bridge is in Daniel Boone National Forest. From the Mountain Parkway, take KY 11 to Natural Bridge State Park. For information call (606) 663–2214.

FAMILY FEUD

The longest feud in U.S. history belongs to Kentucky. No, I'm not talking about the Hatfields and McCoys. They settled their dispute long ago, after a few decades of squabbling. I'm talking about Brownie, Kentucky's Everly Brothers, Don and Phil, early rock-and-roll stars who had huge hits with "Wake Up Little Susie," "Bye-bye Love," and "Cathy's Clown."

But growing up together and singing together and touring together and starting a record label together took its toll. In 1973 Phil smashed his guitar during a concert and walked off the stage, leaving Don to explain to the audience that the two were through. "The Everly Brothers died ten years ago," he announced to the stunned audience.

They reunited in 1983 as a singing duo but not as pals. They still perform on stage together, but lest you think they've left that feud behind, understand that they ride to their performances in separate limos. If the Everly Brothers died in '63, as Don told that audience, then they are about to begin their fifth decade of feuding.

REST FOR THE WEARY SHOESHINE MAN
Slade

Not many shoeshine men have a rest area named after them. Then again, not many shoeshine men *lobby* to have one named after them. Junior Williamson, a native of Pike County, was a shoeshine man at the capitol in Frankfort. Every day he diligently shined the shoes of the state's top politicians. He was known for his humanitarian endeavors, volunteer works, and general all-around good-guy demeanor. Everyone loved Junior.

Junior felt that a rest area was needed near the Slade/Beattyville exit. This particular location was important as it served as the main entrance to the Natural Bridge State Resort Park. So Junior lobbied the politicians each day for its construction as he shined their shoes. And while he was polishing the shoes, he also polished the proverbial apple, suggesting that they could even name it after him.

The Junior Williamson Rest Area is near exit 33 on the Mountain Parkway,

WHERE THEY MILK MORE SNAKES THAN ANY OTHER PLACE IN THE WORLD
Slade

Another 409 snakes arrived at the Kentucky Reptile Zoo in the fall of 2001, bringing the attraction's snake population up to almost 1,500. And these weren't just any snakes. These were deadly Malayan pit vipers imported from Germany in crates marked VENOMOUS.

To most visitors the zoo is just another tourist attraction—"Would you mind posing with one of your distant relatives, Mildred? Ha-ha." But it's also the world's largest supplier of snake venom for medical research. Malayan pit viper venom, for instance, is used in research on drugs to treat stroke victims and sells for about $50 a gram. Sounds like easy money—until you find out it takes about twenty-five snakes to produce about a gram of venom. Easy money if you don't mind "milking" a snake. How do you milk a snake? You'll have to come watch. That's another attraction at the Kentucky Reptile Zoo. Snake milking happens about every two weeks, so call ahead to coordinate your schedule.

The Kentucky Reptile Zoo is located behind the Mountain Parkway's Junior Williamson Rest Area on KY 11. Call (606) 663-9160.

STILL A UNION STRONGHOLD
Vanceburg

Vanceburg is home to the only freestanding monument dedicated to the Union soldiers who fought in the Civil War. This may seem risky for a small, southern town in a state that supported slavery, but diversity is something Vanceburg was founded on.

Vanceburg was settled in 1797 by Moses Baird, who led a group of men to Kentucky in search of riches in the salt-making industry. Baird liked the area he settled in so much that he named it Vanceburg after a friend, Joseph Vance. While much of the state relied on slave labor to work the crops, and thus many supported the Confederates, 107 Vanceburg men died in the war efforts as Union soldiers. A monument was erected in 1884 in their honor. The monument is listed with the National Register of Historic Places as the only Union monument south of the Mason-Dixon line.

Inscribed on the monument is this: "The war for the Union was right, everlastingly right, and the war against the Union was wrong, forever wrong." Then follows the list of the 107 Lewis County Union men killed during the war.

The monument is on the courthouse lawn on Second Street.

COAL MINER'S DAUGHTER

S *he really was a coal miner's daughter. She really was married at thirteen, a mother at fifteen, and a grandmother at twenty-nine. But she made something of her life despite these obstacles.*

Loretta Lynn wouldn't take no for an answer and through sheer force of will—and a lot of shoe leather—became the biggest star in country music during the sixties and seventies. The Kentucky native (born in the tiny town of Butcher Hollow) had a string of hits, some seventy in all during that period, including such hard-edged country songs as "Don't Come Home a Drinkin' (With Lovin' on Your Mind)," "You Ain't Woman Enough (To Take My Man)" and "I'm a Honky Tonk Girl." The girl had an attitude long before it was fashionable.

Her husband, Mooney, once said that the two of them drove 80,000 miles to sell 50,000 copies of her first record in 1959, but it paid off. That song, "I'm a Honky Tonk Girl," made it to Number 14 on the country charts and established Lynn as a star. She would go on to record twenty-six number one country hits.

Born in 1934, Lynn is now collecting Social Security checks along with her royalty checks—and still recording.

THE PENNYRILE

THE PENNYRILE

I wish there were a better story for why the south-central part of the state from the Tennessee River to the Appalachian Mountains is known as the Pennyrile. The name is just the way Kentuckians pronounce, or mispronounce, pennyroyal.

What's a pennyroyal, you ask? From the name you might think that kings and paupers converged to settle the frontiers of south-central Kentucky. And you would be wrong. Actually pennyroyal is a mintlike plant that was once as ubiquitous to the area as kudzu is now. Even the name pennyroyal is a corruption; the proper name, the name herbalists use, is *Pulioll-royall*. Pliny (the Elder, I believe) gave the plant its name. Pulex is Latin for fleas, and Pliny noted how marvelous the plant was at driving the pesky bugs away.

In modern times the main use for pennyroyal has been in an herbal tea that is reputed to relieve gas. The green leaves of the plant are also held in high esteem by bunny breeders because they reduce diarrhea in their rabbits.

I would be willing to bet that most of the people who live in the Pennyrile are unfamiliar with these stories. But it does explain the preponderance of curious stories in the area.

COUNTER CULTURE
Bardstown

Hurst Drugs in Bardstown is a throwback to the old days, when the drug store was more than just a place to get a prescription filled. Part of the charm of the old drug store was the soda fountain. Soda fountains weren't just for lunch. They were for breakfast and midmorning coffee; they were for afternoon smokes and after-school cokes. At the end of World War II, 60 percent of America's drug stores had working soda fountains, according to a 1948 edition of *Remington's Practice of*

While Lana Turner wasn't discovered here, you can discover the best old-fashioned ice cream sodas you've ever had at the soda fountain at Hurst Drugs.

Pharmacy. Not anymore. You have to drive a long ways nowadays to find a drug store soda fountain, but we still have a few in Kentucky. There's Wagner's Pharmacy on Fourth Street in Louisville, a favorite with the jockeys and trainers at nearby Churchill Downs. Smith Pharmacy in Burkesville, the state's oldest drug store, still operates a soda fountain. At Huchinson Drug Store in Lexington's Victorian Square, they still make ice-cream sodas the old-fashioned way.

On my most recent visit to Hurst Drugs, Pat the counter lady fixed me the most perfect grilled-cheese sandwich, with the corners seared, and a vanilla milk shake that made me forswear ever buying another drive-thru shake.

Hurst Drugs is located at 102 North Third Street in Bardstown. The food's good, the service is great, and the friendly customers are tops.

BOURBON INVENTED BY BAPTIST MINISTER!
Bardstown

Oscar Getz didn't invent bourbon. That is generally credited to Elijah Craig—and we thank him for it—a Baptist minister who operated a still in Georgetown, Kentucky, a town that is now dry (alcoholic beverages prohibited), in the 1780s. But isn't that a nifty tabloid headline: Bourbon Invented by Baptist Minister! If only it were true.

But Oscar Getz did invent the Whiskey Museum, sort of. It's called the Oscar Getz Museum of Whiskey History, and it's in the Bourbon Capital of the World, Bardstown, Kentucky, which was at one time home to twenty-two distilleries. As recently as

School field trips were never like this! You can find enough whiskey bottles to decorate a freshman dorm at the Oscar Getz Museum of Whiskey History.

thirty years ago, whiskey distilling was the town's only industry. They've branched out now, into tourism. That's where the Oscar Getz Museum of Whiskey History comes in.

It's there that you can hear the story of Elijah Craig, reputed inventor of bourbon whiskey. Alexis Lichine's *New Encyclopedia of Wines & Spirits* says, "Early in the colonial history of America, a Baptist minister, Elijah Craig, established a still in Georgetown, Kentucky, and began producing whiskey from a base of corn. The still is said to have been one of the first in Kentucky, and customers in neighboring towns christened his product Bourbon County Whiskey, from the county of origin."

It's a great story—they even teach it in Kentucky schools—but it isn't true.

There was an Elijah Craig, and he did distill whiskey. But he didn't do it in Bourbon County. He never lived in Bourbon County. And he wasn't alone as a distiller of spirits; it was a fact of life in pioneer days. The claim for Craig wasn't even made until a century later in Richard Collins's *History of Kentucky,* published in 1874. The first bourbon was most likely distilled in the first Kentucky settlement: Fort Harrod (now Harrodsburg), which was established in 1774. Bourbon County wasn't even established for another fifteen years, and it was named for the reigning royal family of France, the Bourbons.

At that time Bourbon County was the size of thirty-four modern counties. As the legislature carved out more and more counties, the region came to be known as Old Bourbon. So when whiskey was shipped downriver to other areas, it became known as Old Bourbon Whiskey. It was soon recognized as the best—we Kentuckians are good with vices. Customers began demanding Bourbon whiskey. Other whiskey makers latched onto the name and, voila, bourbon whiskey was born.

You can hear that story and see enough whiskey bottles to decorate a freshman dorm at the Oscar Getz Museum of Whiskey History. And find out about Oscar Getz, who didn't invent bourbon whiskey, either, but was a great student of the brand. His family owned the old Tom Moore Distillery in Bardstown, and Getz developed a taste for his subject, studying whiskey's history and collecting anything and everything bourbon related. He lectured on the subject in the fifties and sixties, and after his death in 1983 his widow donated his collection to the city of Bardstown, which opened it to the world in this museum of whiskey.

Sorry, no free samples.

The Oscar Getz Museum of Whiskey History is in Spalding Hall at 114 North Fifth Street. For information call (502) 348-2999. Admission is free.

WHERE JOHN FITCH, INVENTOR OF THE STEAMBOAT, DID HIMSELF IN

J *ohn Fitch wasn't born in Kentucky—he was born in Connecticut in 1743—but he died here. Fitch had a tough childhood and an unhappy marriage. But he also had a dream, and in 1782 he moved to Pennsylvania with a grand scheme: to build a steamboat.*

He was able to secure financial backing from private investors to pursue his newfound obsession. In 1790 Fitch completed the first successful steamboat passenger run between Philadelphia and Trenton, New Jersey. No one paid too much attention to the fact that the boat could only reach speeds of 6 to 8 miles per hour. Instead most people laughed at the design. Resembling a long canoe, the steamboat had six oars on each side, powered by a steam engine. Those who did not laugh at the contraption feared it. They were scared that stepping foot on board Fitch's steamboat would be the last step they took. Needless to say, it was a hard sell to the public. Fitch went back to the drawing board and replaced the oars with giant paddles. It didn't work—and it still scared the masses.

Fitch eventually called it quits and fled to Bardstown for the sole purpose of killing himself. Fitch made a deal with the local innkeeper: For an exchange of 150 acres of land, the innkeeper agreed to house Fitch and give him one pint of whiskey a day. Drinking himself to death didn't work, so Fitch gave the innkeeper another 150 acres of land and upped the ante to two pints of whiskey a day. It still didn't work. Fitch was a failure at suicide. Not wanting to waste any more time—plus he had run out of land to give away—Fitch finally overdosed on opium in his Bardstown room.

LUCKY 13 HOUSE
Bardstown

F ederal Hill, Judge John Rowan's plantation house in Bardstown, takes the number 13 to an extreme. There are thirteen
windows, 13-inch-thick walls, thirteen steps in each of the four
staircases, thirteen mantles, thirteen railings on each landing,
thirteen earthquake-protection bars, and 13-foot-high ceilings.
That's because Rowan, who was everything from Kentucky secretary of state to United States senator, believed thirteen was a
lucky number.

It has been for some who've stayed there—Stephen Foster,
for example. Legend has it that Foster stayed here in 1828
while visiting his cousins, the rowdy Rowan kids. Legend also
has it that he composed "My Old Kentucky Home" at the
Rowan family piano and wrote it down at the family desk.
Good legends, but no one can prove them.

The house has proved not so lucky for others, including the
sixteen persons who died from cholera here in 1833.

If you are an aspiring songwriter, interested in penning
state anthems (Foster wrote Kentucky's and Florida's), by all
means check it out. Thirteen could be lucky for you. If you
believe otherwise, don't go.

Federal Hill is located on U.S. 150 just east of downtown.
For tour information call (502) 348–3502.

MORE THAN A CAKE MIX—DUNCAN HINES'S HOMETOWN
Bowling Green

Duncan Hines was the Zagat of his time. A printing salesman by trade, he roamed the country, taste-testing roadside diners from Maine to Miami, from the Atlantic to the Pacific. He first collected his comments in a handy-dandy foldout guide, which he included with his Christmas cards in 1934. His friends and family were so appreciative that he began publishing a regular guide, which he called *Adventures in Good Eating*. Each year it got bigger and fatter—and more popular.

Soon he wasn't selling printing on his travels; he was selling himself, in particular the Duncan Hines Seal of Approval. This sign became a guidepost for hungry travelers. If a restaurant had Hines's approval, that meant two things: It was good, and it was clean.

Soon Hines was so famous that Proctor & Gamble asked him to lend his name to a cake mix. He tested the mix, approved, and signed on. It's been four decades since the last edition of *Adventures in Good Eating*, and not many folks know Duncan Hines from restaurant reviews anymore. But the cake mix . . . we approve!

Two restaurants survive from Hines's first travel guide of 1934: the Beaumont Inn in Harrodsburg and the Shakertown Inn in Pleasant Hill.

Each June Hines's hometown of Bowling Green celebrates his gustatory work with the Duncan Hines Festival—a weekend of good friends, good fun, and, oh yes, good food.

For festival information call (270) 782–0800.

RETURN TO KENTUCKY

*H*ere's a scary thought: John Carpenter is from Kentucky.
Carpenter, who was raised in Bowling Green, wrote and
directed the horror classic Halloween, as well as such other cult
classics as Escape from New York, They Live! and Starman.

Carpenter brought movie violence out of the closet and into
the frame. His breakthrough film Halloween actually showed
blood! Carpenter's tools of horror have long since been surpassed
by bloodier, gorier fare. Watch Halloween today and you may be
surprised about how little gore there is. It's just that in 1978,
most mainstream movie audiences thought of Hitchcock when
they thought of horror, and Hitchcock seldom showed blood.

All this pioneering work was from a guy who almost became
a musician. You see, what brought Carpenter to Kentucky was
music. His father moved the family from Carthage,
New York, to Kentucky when he took a job
heading the music department of Western
Kentucky University. You can see the
musical influence in Carpenter's
films—or hear it actually. He has
written the score for sixteen of
his nineteen films. Including, as
you might expect, Halloween.

DUCKTAIL CAR
Bowling Green

I f you don't now or never did sport a ducktail (or if you are
female and you never hung on the arm of a ducktail-sporting
male), then you may want to skip this site. But if you understand the symbiotic relationship between men, their hair, and
their cars, then you'll want to visit the Corvette Museum, the
only museum in the world devoted to that flashy sports car.

The museum is in Kentucky not because we had more duck-
tails or Corvette's per capita but because we are where it all
started. Kentucky is where every Corvette has been made, and
since they've all been manufactured in Bowling Green, it's only
fitting that the city be the site of the museum.

There's a big anniversary celebration every year, and Cor-
vettes—and their owners—drive in from all over the country.
You'll think you've gone back to the future.

While you are touring the museum, you can also check out
the Corvette Hall of Fame. Sure, if you aren't a Corvette fanatic
you might not recognize the names. But be aware: If you don't
bow in front of the Harley Earl plaque, people may whisper.
You see, Harley was the father of the Corvette. After watching
Jaguars and MGs race at Watkins Glen, he was convinced that
America needed its own sports car. The tough part was convincing General Motors. But he managed to convince Ed Cole
(another Hall of Famer) at GM's traditional "bow-tie" division,
Chevrolet, and the rest would become history.

The National Corvette Museum is at 350 Corvette Drive,
Bowling Green, Kentucky 42101. Call (270) 781–7973 or (800)
53–VETTE ('53 was, of course, the year of the first 'Vette).

WORLD'S LARGEST HAM & BISCUIT
Cadiz

This one will give you heartburn just from reading about it: a two-ton ham biscuit. That's not a misprint. That's four thousand pounds of country ham and biscuit. And it's not a one-time thing. They've been baking this breakfast monstrosity every year since 1985 as part of Cadiz's Trigg County Country Ham Festival.

The Trigg pig gig every October swells this small town on the Tennessee border from 4,000 folks to 80,000 ham-lovers. That's a far cry from Farm-City Week, the event's predecessor, which was highlighted by a baking contest. In 1977 some Trig-gians put their heads together and realized this baking contest didn't really make sense since Trigg County had long been known for its hams not its baked goods. So they created the Country Ham Festival—and it's been growing every year.

They cook up a 720-pound biscuit in a custom-built 500,000 BTU oven, then lay on a little more than 3,000 pounds of cured pork. The biscuit was blessed by the *Guinness Book of World Records,* which had no previous record holder in that category (didn't have that category either).

The big biscuit isn't the only reason to attend Trigg's pig jig. There's a mess of small town fair-type events, including a pig derby, a greased pig–catching contest, and a kiss-a-pig competition. Don't worry if you get drafted into the latter event. Pigs don't kiss back.

For more information call the Cadiz-Trigg County Tourist Commission at (888) 446–6402.

BIRTH OF THE BAPTISTS
Cane Ridge

The Baptists were born in Kentucky—along with the Methodists, the Disciples of Christ, the Pentecostals, the Holy Rollers, virtually every religion that depends on a fervor from its congregation.

Okay, they weren't literally born here; they were all founded elsewhere. But an event on the Kentucky prairie two centuries ago rejuvenated what had been fringe religions. It happened in 1801 in the Cane Ridge Meeting House, a meeting hall that is said to be the largest one-room log building in North America today, measuring 40 by 60 feet.

Paul Conkin, former head of the history department at Vanderbilt University and author of *Cane Ridge: America's Pentecost* (and my first cousin, I should note, in the interest of full disclosure), calls the meeting at Cane Ridge "the most important religious gathering in all of American history, both for what it symbolized and the effects that flowed from it."

More than 20,000 people gathered around that log building in August 1801 to hear preachers and orators and fire-and-brimstone sermons. Many lay down on the ground and shook from their newborn religious fervor. Hands were laid on, offerings were collected, souls were given over. It was one phenomenal gathering: For six days that tiny spot was Kentucky's largest city. One eyewitness, James Finley, wrote in his biography that "the noise was like the roar of Niagara. At one time I saw at least 500 swept down in a moment as if a battery of a thousand guns had been opened upon them, and then immediately followed shrieks and shouts that rent the very heavens."

But it was more than a religious revival; it was also a social gathering, the first in the new state's history (Kentucky was a mere nine years old). Some souls weren't just saved, they were married. Nine months after Cane Ridge, Kentucky experienced its first baby boom.

The Old Cane Ridge Meeting House is 8 miles east of Paris, Kentucky. Take U.S. 460 East to KY 537. For information call (859) 987–5350.

THE WORLD'S FIRST MEDIA EVENT
Cave City

Floyd Collins was just born under a bad sign. Although he had great luck finding and exploring caves, he never could seem to profit from them.

At the height of the great "cave wars" of the 1920s, everyone but Collins seemed to prosper and receive vast wealth, even though he was the principal cave discoverer at the time. Many cave owners paid Collins to explore their caves, searching for new caverns, domes, and anything else that would attract more tourists. They hired Collins not only because he knew the caves in the Kentucky area better than anyone else, but because he was fearless—that, and he needed the money.

Collins owned a cave himself, Great Crystal Cave, but nearly went bankrupt. No one came to visit his cave because it was off the beaten track. Mammoth Cave was the area's biggest draw, and it left the smaller caverns clamoring for the public's attention. Some cave owner's hired street performers to get the attention of travelers passing by. Some used more persuasive techniques by spreading rumors about "unfortunate" occurrences in other caves.

Cave owner George Morrison had a brilliant idea that set him apart from the rest. Morrison decided to build a new entrance to his cave that would link it to Mammoth Cave, opening the floodgates for tourists. He called it the "New Entrance to Mammoth Cave," and it worked. People began visiting Morrison's cave in droves.

Collins saw the potential in Morrison's idea, and on January 30, 1925, he set out in Sand Cave with the intention of somehow linking his cave to Morrison's, thus being able to share the new entrance and finally getting the tourist dollars he had dreamed about. But as with everything else in his life, Collins would find himself out of luck. While in a crawl space that was so tight he couldn't put his hand between his chest and the wall, Collins kicked a rock, trapping his leg. News of Collins's predicament captivated the nation. Finally he had made news—front page news, no less, with more than sixteen newspapers sending reporters to cover the saga. The world read with anticipation, following all the details of how Collins was doing and the progress at freeing him. People wanted him to win!

Not only had Collins's luck turned with the media, but his financial luck also prospered. Tourists flooded his Great Crystal Cave in record numbers. Someone had to feed all the tourists and media. Collins's family set up a hamburger restaurant near the entrance so that people could grab a bite to eat while waiting and watching. His family prospered further by selling souvenirs, everything from shirts to key chains, to mugs—all commemorating Collins' ill fortune, physically anyway.

It all came to an end, though, after sixteen days. Rescue workers were unable to free Collins, and he died in the cave from exposure to the elements. Some of the townspeople who knew Collins said that dying was the best thing that ever happened to him. After years of missed success, fame, and fortune, he finally found it. He just didn't get to enjoy it.

The Floyd Collins Museum is inside the Wayfarer Bed and Breakfast, 1240 Old Mammoth Cave Road. Call (270) 773–3366.

TACKY TOWN USA

Welcome to Cave City! Home of Mammoth Cave, Diamond Cavern, and cement statues.

While some may balk at the tackiness of Cave City, for the more adventurous tourist, Cave City is trash heaven! In addition to boasting the world's largest cave system, Cave City also has more cement-statuary stores and miniature-golf parks than any other city in the country. The number is evenly divided, with either one or the other on every corner.

Everyone can be pleased with a stop at Cave City. Need a gift for that hard-to-shop-for person? Pick up a 5-foot-tall cement statue of a rooster. Tired of being nagged by the kids with an endless banter of "Are we there yet?" Stretch your legs out at Jellystone Park, Cave City's "amusement" park, complete with waterslides. Jellystone also makes a perfect photo op. You guessed it—they have a giant cement statue of Yogi Bear! If you prefer more adventurous amusement, stop at Guntown Mountain Amusement Park and see live gunfights (staged, of course) and saloon shows.

Still not convinced that Cave City is for you? Try one of their fine-dining restaurants. Joe's Diner is nestled in a metallic boxcar. The Sahara Steakhouse is right next to the Mammoth Cave Wildlife Museum, which features a display of animals found inside the caves and is also Kentucky's first and largest wildlife museum.

If those stops don't quite whet your appetite for Cave City, perhaps you'd be interested in the handful of antiques malls, craft stores, and "odd ball" gift shops the town has to offer. Where else would you be able to find a 15-foot-tall knight? Yes, a knight in shining armor. He stands next to a 15-foot-high totem pole that can be yours as well.

Competition for the tourist dollar is fierce in Cave City. In fact, you'd be hard pressed to find a store that didn't combine one or more of the more notable selling items in the city. You can buy gas and a cement statue of a gorilla at the truck stop. Mammoth Cave Wax Museum also sells rocks. And Diamond Caverns has branched out into antiques as well as guided tours. The list is endless. You'll just have to stop and immerse yourself in the culture of tack for its full appreciation.

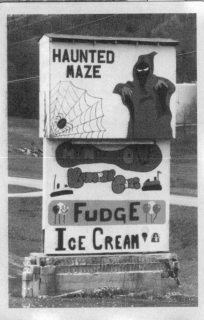

One-stop shopping. No doubt about it, you can find something for everyone on your Christmas list at Cave City.

A Machine Gun by Any Other Name . . .

*I*f it weren't for Kentuckian John Thompson, military men everywhere would be walking around carrying a Blish Gun. And how intimidating would that be? But fortunately it was Thompson who worked out most of the weapon details on the submachine gun and thus lent it his name, the Tommy gun!

In 1914 Thompson retired from the Army and began working full-time developing a lightweight personal gun that would fire bullets at a rapid pace. He was driven by two goals: One, to make lots of money and two, to end the war in Europe. Thompson felt that if our boys had a small machine gun with rapid-fire ability, the war would quickly be over. He worked hard at developing the gun, but he came across a stumbling block. In order for the gun to work properly, it needed a simple lock, called a breech lock.

While researching patent files he found a patent under the name of Navy Commander John Bell Blish, who had invented such a lock, known as the "Blish lock." In 1915 Thompson and Blish began working together. Blish agreed to let Thompson use his lock in exchange for a stock in an arms company Thompson planned to start. And he didn't insist that the Blish lock be used on the Blish gun. In the spring of 1916 Thompson received financial backing from Thomas Fortune Ryan, a tobacco tycoon, and he began Auto Ordinance Corporation.

In 1918 his company invented the Annihilator I, a machine gun that lived up to its name: It could empty a twenty-round magazine in less than a second. Thompson thought he had struck gold, but as luck would have it the first shipment of Tommy guns destined for the war effort in Europe arrived at the New York docks on November 11, 1918—the day the war ended. Thompson decided that since the war effort was a bust, he'd redesign the gun for personal use because, hey, everyone needs a machine gun. The first public demonstration of the personal submachine gun was in August 1920. By 1925 anyone with $225 could buy a Tommy gun at the local participating hardware store. And how many would have been sold if it had been called the Blish gun?

WIGWAM VILLAGE
Cave City

Look! It's a wigwam! No, actually it's a tepee.

Frank Redford had a dream—a dream not of wealth, love, or world peace, but rather of a village built entirely of tepees where people could come together and experience a sense of community Indian style. Actually, in the dream it was a village built of upside-down ice-cream cones. Being the visionary he was—and knowing that a town made of food was nearly impossible—he

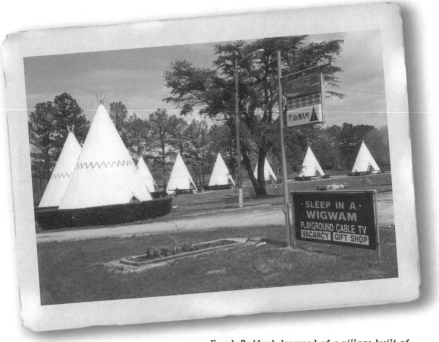

Frank Redford dreamed of a village built of upside-down ice-cream cones—but had the sense to know that a town made of food was nearly impossible. So he built Wigwam Village instead.

decided to equate the geometric shape he was seeking with a tepee. It all worked out in the end.

In 1935 Redford built Wigwam Village in Horse Cave, Kentucky. You may be wondering, what exactly is a wigwam village? The village served more as a motel than actual tepee. The wigwam offered families a unique place to sleep, complete with the comforts of home, minus the phones and television. All the wigwams, built of steel and concrete, were set in a circular pattern opening to a "community center" where kids could play and parents could relax. Kind of like a tepee utopia.

Wigwam Village was a success! So in 1937 Redford patented the idea and built five more villages—in Alabama, Florida, Louisiana, California, and Arizona. However, the popularity of the wigwam villages didn't last. There are only two left, the one in Cave City and one in Holbrook, Arizona.

From I–65, take exit 53 (Cave City) to KY 90 East, then north on 31W about 1.5 miles. The village is at 601 North Dixie Highway. Call (270) 773–3381.

HAPPY DAYS FESTIVAL
Corydon

Yes, there is a parade. No, Fonzie is not the grand marshal. Every year Corydon comes alive on the Fourth of July to celebrate the Happy Days Festival. Corydon actually had no interest in creating a festival to compete with other counties and cities. The city really didn't have a need to celebrate anything at all. However, in the early 1990s Crawford Park was donated to the city, although at the time of its donation it wasn't much of a park. Through volunteer efforts and fund-raising it became one. Not really knowing what to do with their park, the natives decided it would be a great place to have a festival and continue the fund-raising efforts and volunteer spirit.

Now that they had their very own festival they needed a name. There is no animal native to Corydon, nor is there a fruit, vegetable, or music style. Corydon's big claim to fame is that a former Kentucky governor was born there, but he wasn't just any governor. He was Albert Benjamin "Happy" Chandler, former baseball commissioner. Thus, the event was named the Happy Days Festival.

What will you find at the Happy Days Festival? World-famous ugly women. Corydon is known for their Womenless contest, where male notables of the city dress in drag to compete for the title of ugliest woman. You'll also find a parade of antique cars, mules, and wagons—and a heaping supply of barbecue.

For more information contact the Kentucky Department of Travel at (800) 225-8747.

THUMB PICKERS HALL OF FAME
Drakesboro

There are all kinds of pickers out there, and while Kentucky may have its fair share of class-act nose pickers, it is (understandably) the thumb picker they choose to celebrate.

The National Thumb Picker's Hall of Fame is located in Muhlenberg County. Thumb picking is a unique style of guitar playing, where the fingers play the melody of the song and the thumb plays the bass. Done correctly, it resembles the sound of two guitars playing at one time.

This style of picking was initially made famous by Central City, Kentucky, native and country music legend Merle Travis. Muhlenberg County is so proud of their picking son that every year they have a birthday bash on November 27. The tribute includes thumb picking contests and sixty gallons of beef stew served with corn bread and peach or apple cobbler, Merle's favorite meal.

For more information call the Central City/Muhlenberg County Chamber of Commerce at (270) 754-2360.

I'D LIKE TO TEACH THE WORLD TO . . .
COLLECT COCA-COLA MEMORABILIA
Elizabethtown

Newsflash: A Kentucky couple holds what is the world's largest privately owned collection of Coca-Cola memorabilia. There's really no competition other than the Coca-Cola Company itself in Atlanta, and that's not exactly "Privately Owned."

The Schmidts come by their Coke obsession naturally: The family has been an official Coca-Cola bottler since 1901. The collecting thing got started in the early 1970s with Jan and Bill Schmidt, who started collecting advertising memorabilia. It took off, and pretty soon the Schmidts had it all—from Coca-Cola serving trays to Coca-Cola calendars, drinking glasses, knives, playing cards, coolers, vending machines, ancient bottling equipment, toys, sheet music, and, oh yes, Coca-Cola bottles, of which there are many styles.

You can't stroll through the collection without saying, "Oh, I remember that." The Schmidts like it when you say that; it means they've done their job.

The Schmidts are looking for a location to display their collection, but for now it's not for public consumption.

WHERE JIMI HENDRIX BROKE HIS ANKLE
Fort Knox

It's probably more famous as the place where all the gold is. But some of us prefer to think of it as the place where Jimi Hendrix broke his ankle while in basic training. It's Fort Knox, home of the Bullion Depository.

As surprising as it may seem, a bullion depository is not where they store soup broth. The Bullion Depository in Fort Knox is actually where our nation houses the largest amount of U.S. gold reserves. The depository was completed in December 1936 and was in use by January 1937 by the U.S. Mint. More than 750 tons of reinforced steel surrounded by 670 tons of structural steel helps keep the gold bars safe—not to mention the vault doors that weigh more than twenty tons each.

In addition to being one of the safest places on earth, the depository is equipped with its own emergency power plant, water system, and shooting range in the basement—so that the guards can keep in top form. No one is allowed down in the depository itself, but you can view it from a second-level overlook area. Each gold bar inside is worth approximately $16,000. No single person has the combination to the safe. Instead, several people have a combination and for the doors to open, each one must put his or her code in.

Fort Knox isn't only home to the nation's largest warehouse of gold; it also houses the largest U.S. Army museum. On January 16, 1932, the First Cavalry Regiment, the Army's oldest mounted unit, relocated to Fort Knox and left their horses behind. The Armored Forces began in July 1940. The General George Smith Patton Jr. Museum opened in 1949, proudly displaying the nation's progression of weaponry throughout the ages. Today Fort Knox has the largest collection of tanks, guns, and Army machinery in the free world—also gold.

Call (502) 624–3812 for information. No visitors are allowed at the Bullion Depository, but you can visit the Patton Museum at 554 Fayette Avenue (near the Chaffee Avenue entrance to Ft. Knox). Take Chaffee Avenue east off Dixie Highway (U.S. 31). Turn left on Ballard, then left on Fayette. The museum's phone number is (502) 943–8977.

KENTUCKY'S FIRST UFO
Fort Knox

The UFO sighting craze that began in Roswell, New Mexico, in 1947 arrived in Kentucky shortly after New Year's Day 1948. Tower control at Godman Air Force Base in Fort Knox picked up an unidentified flying object on its radar on January 7, 1948, and sent Captain Charles Mantrell scrambling in his P–51 jet. As Mantrell approached the UFO, he radioed back: "It appears to be a metallic object . . . tremendous in size . . . directly ahead and slightly above . . . I am trying to close for a better look."

That was the last transmission received from Mantrell. He crashed his plane and died, and no one knows to this day if what he saw was a genuine UFO or another of those ubiquitous weather balloons.

Fort Knox is located on U.S. 31W just south of Louisville, but don't try to get too close. That's where all the gold is, too, so they aren't exactly receptive to tourists. But you can look up in the skies south of the base and imagine what it must have been like that cold January day in 1948 when the first UFO was spotted in Kentucky.

THE TOBACCO STATE—BIRTHPLACE OF THE NICOTINE PATCH
Franklin

There's no irony here, not much. Kentucky, land of tobacco, is also home to the man who invented a product to help smokers kick their cigarette habit.

Franklin native Dr. Frank Etscorn graduated from Western Kentucky University in 1973 with a master's degree in experimental psychology. Etscorn developed the nicotine patch as a fluke: He accidentally spilled liquid nicotine on his arm while working on a research project at New Mexico Tech. A nonsmoker, Etscorn's eyes lit up. Just that brief skin contact gave him the sensation of having smoked a pack of cigarettes. That's when the idea hit him of inventing a patch that could feed nicotine through the skin, helping addicts kick the habit. Etscorn toiled on the product, perfected it, and sold it to a pharmaceutical company, making a fortune in the process. In 1992 both *Time* and *Fortune* magazines named the nicotine patch one of the best new products of the year.

Etscorn has been working on a number of important research projects, including a method to thwart termites by treating lumber with hot chili peppers.

A TALE OF
TWO PRESIDENTS

*T*he debate has raged for many years: Is it the Civil War or the War Between the States? In Kentucky we have our own answer: It should be called the War Within the State. That's because in 1861 the president of the country, no matter your sympathies, was a Kentuckian. The president of the United States of America, Abraham Lincoln, had been born near Hodgenville. The president of the Confederate States of America, Jefferson Davis, had been born in Fairview, not far from Paducah.

The largest cast-concrete monument in the United States marks the spot of Davis's birth in Fairview on June 3, 1808. He lived in the Bluegrass State only two years but came back for school (St. Thomas of Aquinas Catholic School in Springfield) and college (Transylvania College in Lexington) before shipping out to attend the U.S. Military Academy at West Point in New York in 1824. He even married a Kentucky girl, Sarah Knox Taylor, daughter of his commanding officer, General Zachary Taylor, but she died three months later of malaria.

Davis had a distinguished career—Mexican War hero, a congressman and senator from Mississippi, Secretary of War under Franklin Pierce—until he cast his lot with the losing side in the Civil War.

At a Confederate reunion in 1907, one of his generals, Simon Bolivar Buckner, suggested a monument to honor Davis. The result is a 351-foot-tall obelisk resting on a foundation of Kentucky limestone. The monument looks startlingly similar to the Washington Monument, but don't mention that. Folks around here don't want to hear it.

The Davis Monument is one of seventy-two Confederate monuments in the state, compared with only two Union ones—this despite the fact that Kentucky sent three times as many troops to the Union as to the Confederacy and was officially neutral during the Civil War. Or is that the War Between the States?

The Jefferson Davis Monument State Historic Site is 9 miles east of Hopkinsville on U.S. 68. For more information call (270) 886-1765.

PENN'S STORE'S GREAT OUTHOUSE
BLOWOUT AND RACE
Gravel Switch

This is exactly what it sounds like. People mount outhouses (an outhouse is an outdoor bathroom, for the uninitiated) on wheels and race them down the road. The winner gets, uh, the honor of being known as the winner. The event, which lasts four days, is held every October.

But it's worth visiting Penn's Store even if you visit out of outhouse season. That's because the store is the oldest in the country in continuous operation by the same family. Gabriel Jackson Penn bought the place in 1850 (it had been in business since at least 1845), renamed it Penn's Store, and it's been in the Penn family ever since.

The Outhouse Race is a recent addition. The Penn people started it in 1992 when the store got its first outhouse. That's right, the place had been operating for 142 years without a bathroom. But there are a lot of nice, big trees nearby.

There's more to the Great Outhouse Blowout than outhouse racing; there's also fiddling, whittling, a gathering of herb enthusiasts, and the much-anticipated Parade of Privies.

Penn's Store is at 257 Penn's Store Road in Gravel Switch, Phone (859) 332–7715 or (859) 332–7706.

The Penn people caution that their place is not easy to find. Here's their directions from the Renfro Valley exit on I–75: "Turn left onto Highway 461 and follow until it intersects with Highway 150. Turn west (right) onto Highway 150. At Stanford, turn left onto Highway 27. Then turn right onto Highway 150 again and go through downtown Stanford. Turn west (left) onto Highway 78. Turn north (right) onto Highway 243.

Follow for approximately 6 miles. Just before Highway 243 intersects with Highway 37, turn left onto a side road. Penn's Store is straight ahead." It's next to a popular swimming hole, where the Little South Creek meets North Rolling Fork.

COW DAYS
Greensburg

Technically it's the Greensburg Rotary Club—Double Cola/Ski Cow Days Festival. But everybody around Greensburg just calls it Cow Days.

It really isn't that exciting. Unless you are a cow. Just the usual small-town festival stuff: food vendors, arts and crafts competitions, an antique tractor show, a frog-croaking contest (but not a cow-mooing contest), a pipe-smoking contest, a cow giveaway, and a flea market. And they take their flea market seriously. The vendor contract specifies: "We will not allow anyone to sell Snap-Pops, Smelly Gas, Hair Color Spray, or any other object considered offensive by the Greensburg Rotary Club." Kind of makes you want to buy a can of Smelly Gas, doesn't it?

But you have to admit, Cow Days is a great name for a festival.

Cow Days is held every September. For more information call (270) 932–4298.

Quintessential Kentuckians
The High Lonesome Sound of Bill Monroe

*E*lvis may have been the King of Rock and Roll, but he wasn't its father. Neither was Louis Armstrong the father of jazz. But as sure as can be, Bill Monroe was the father of bluegrass. Monroe, born in tiny Rosine, Kentucky, in 1911, invented the musical form, gave it its name, and was its embodiment until his death in 1996.

Monroe started out in a conventional country band with his brothers, Charlie and Birch. In the early thirties the three worked at an East Chicago oil refinery during the week and played house parties on the weekends. They even danced (yes, danced!) on the WLS radio "Barn Dance" some weekends. Such was the financial structure of country music at the time that its finest musicians had to square dance and hold day jobs to pay the bills. Country music was essentially a regional music, and record sales were definitely not in the Garth Brooks range.

Birch left the band in 1934 when the boys landed a sponsor, a laxative company, that wanted them to move to Iowa. Bill and Charlie continued performing, eventually recording for Bluebird Records. But despite their brotherly love, the two didn't get along. Charlie, eight years older, gregarious, and domineering, was the lead singer and the group leader. Bill, who was born with crossed eyes and poor vision, was a loner with a bit of a chip on his shoulder. They couldn't even agree on the direction their music should take, so they split in 1938. Charlie kept the recording contract; Bill got his musical independence.

He formed an all-string band, where the emphasis was on the instruments. The vocals, usually performed by Bill, were tight with what he called a "high lonesome sound." He first called the gang Bill Monroe and the Kentuckians, later changing the name to Bill Monroe and the Blue Grass Boys. They played church-style harmonies to a dance beat with hints of blues and jazz. Their big break came when they played an upbeat version of Jimmie Rodgers's "Mule Skinner Blues" on the Grand Ole Opry. Their reputation, and bluegrass music's appeal, were formed.

Over the years Monroe's band was a virtual training school for future bluegrass legends, including Flatt and Scruggs, Reno and Smiley, Chubby Wise, Carter Stanley, Mac Wiseman, and Vassar Clements. Monroe's musical virtuosity attracted these young musicians, and his prickly personality forced them out on their own—a devil's bargain that kept bluegrass music fresh.

LAWYER LINCOLN'S FIRST CASE . . .
DEFENDING HIMSELF!
Hawesville

The Lincolns were living on Pigeon Creek in Indiana in 1827 when eighteen-year-old Abe took a job at nearby Posey's Landing, running a ferryboat across the Anderson River, which empties into the Ohio. Looking to make a little money on the side, Abe built a rowboat and took to ferrying passengers out to the paddle wheelers that steamed up and down the Ohio.

The Dill brothers, who operated a ferry across the Ohio in Kentucky, thought Abe was stealing some of their business. They had an exclusive license to operate a ferryboat across the river at that spot, and they convinced the local constable, Squire Samuel Pate, to haul young Abe up on charges of operating an illegal ferryboat.

The *Commonwealth of Kentucky vs. Abraham Lincoln* was tried in Pate's home at Little Yellow Banks across the river from Troy, Indiana, near the future site of Hawesville in the spring of 1827. After hearing the charge, Lincoln argued that his boat did not cross the river. And if it didn't cross the river, it couldn't be a ferry, so he didn't need a license. Squire Pate was impressed with Lincoln's presentation and logic and dismissed the case. But he also advised Lincoln that he should familiarize himself with the law before he got into any new businesses.

Lincoln took the constable's words at face value. He began reading his friend David Turnham's *Revised Laws of Indiana* and made frequent forays back across the Ohio to observe the proceedings in Pate's court. Seven years later, after election to the Illinois legislature, Lincoln took up formal study of the law; in 1836 he was licensed to practice in Illinois.

Pate House is located 3 miles west of Hawesville on Kentucky Highway 334. Lincoln's case was tried in the east room of the log house.

"M" Is for the Money We Spend on Mother's Day Each Year
Henderson

Mary Wilson was a teacher at the Henderson School in 1887 when she got the idea to have her students honor their mothers. They put together a musical program, called it their Mother's Day Musical, and invited all their moms to the schoolhouse to watch. It quickly became an annual event, and Mrs. Wilson was traveling to other local schools to help them with their musical celebrations.

She didn't live to see her little celebration declared a national holiday in 1916. In one of the ironies of life, Mary Wilson was never a mother. She died in childbirth.

It should be noted that West Virginia disputes this story, claiming Mother's Day as the invention of Anna Maria Reeves Jarvis, of Grafton, West Virginia, who founded the Mother's Day Work Clubs, which provided domestic help for mothers with tuberculosis. Jarvis organized many mothers' celebrations in her life and lobbied President Woodrow Wilson to make Mother's Day a holiday. She convinced her minister to conduct a Mother's Day service on May 12, 1907, and this is recognized everywhere else as the first Mother's Day celebration in the United States.

In Kentucky, we know better. Mary Wilson invented Mother's Day two decades earlier.

The Henderson School was at the corner of Green and Center Streets. Mary Wilson lived for many years at 232 South Main Street in what is now known as the Towles-Sasseen House.

HAIRCUTTING IN FOUR-PART HARMONY
Hodgenville

Admit it, you thought a barbershop quartet was just a bunch of guys with fake mustaches and striped shirts harmonizing at the local Rotary Club luncheon. But there is a real barbershop quartet, as well as a quintet and, on a good day, a sextet. It's at Jackie Jones Barbershop on Lincoln Boulevard in downtown Hodgenville.

Jones is a guitar picker from way back, so it's not unusual for some of his musician friends to drop by on a Saturday afternoon and a hoedown to break out. But it's not "Sweet Adeline," or any other familiar barbershop quartet song, that emerges from the random pluckings of three guitars and a banjo. "Sometimes we play country, sometimes bluegrass. We never know," says Jones. The joint jumps so much that the music spills out onto the street.

They never know when the jamming mood will strike at Jones's shop. So a visitor can't plan a trip to catch this barbershop quartet, which on some days is a trio and on others a quintet or sextet. "It's like breathing," says Jones. "We don't know when we're going to do that either. But we know we're going to do it."

If you didn't bring your instrument, Jackie will fish one out for you. There's a couple of acoustic guitars hanging on the wall, a fiddle dangling above the sink, an electric guitar slid

Music to my ears. On some days, you can get much more than a
shave and a haircut at Jackie Jones Barbershop.

under the front bench, and a steel guitar pushed up against
the wall. Need a banjo? There's a couple of those in the back.
"We keep enough fiddles and guitars around that if somebody
comes by, we got something for them to play," says Jones.

And don't worry if you break a string. Jackie has a few of
those, too—on a shelf above the sink, near the Lucky Tiger hair
tonic. "They tried to get me to license this place as a music
store," he says, "but I already pay $55.50 in taxes. So this stays
a barbershop . . . that happens to have a few musical supplies."

The barbershop is on North Main Street in downtown Hodgenville. Just look for the red-and-white revolving pole. Sorry,
no phone.

LINCOLN'S BOYHOOD HOME . . . SORT OF . . . MAYBE

Hodgenville

Kentucky's license plates should say LAND OF LINCOLN. After all, he was born here, his people were from here, and his best friends lived here. Instead Kentucky's plates read BLUE-GRASS STATE. Illinois gets to call itself the "Land of Lincoln."

It could have been different—except that Kentucky and Lincoln have had a troubled history, going back to his first legal case: defending himself against Kentucky, which was charging him with operating a ferry illegally.

They later tore down the cabin he was born in. That was in 1870, and the place had been nothing more than a corncrib for years. You see, in 1870 Lincoln was not yet a Kentucky legend. There was that Union thing. And while Kentucky was divided about secession and the Civil War, it was not divided about Lincoln. Didn't like him. Not one bit. Gave him a mere 1 percent of the state's vote in the 1860 presidential election. So when the family that owned the Knob Creek farm where the Lincolns had once lived tore down the cabin in 1870, there wasn't one word of protest.

His birthplace—a tiny one-room log cabin 10 miles to the west—we tore that down long before he even made it to Washington. Who knew? So what you will see on the site of his birth and the site of his boyhood home are "symbolic" cabins.

Let's begin at the beginning. Abraham Lincoln was born in a log cabin on Sinking Creek Farm on February 12, 1809. Go to the birth site today and you can see that cabin—or at least what has been billed, off and on, for a century as the log cabin of his birth. There's absolutely no proof that it is. In fact the Park Service hands out a brochure that notes, "Although its early history is obscure, extensive research suggests that the

cabin displayed in the Memorial Building is not the birthplace
of Abraham Lincoln." What it is is a cabin that was constructed
in 1861 from a decaying log house that sat on the old Lincoln
farm site. There may even be a few logs from the original. No
one really knows.

In 1894 a New York restaurateur bought the 1861 cabin and
sent it on tour around the country, exhibiting it in Buffalo,
Nashville, even New York's Central Park. The thing was disas-
sembled and put in storage on Long Island, then rescued in
1900 by Mark Twain and a group of celebrities, who raised the
money to buy the logs and ship them back to Kentucky.

In 1911 the 18-by-16-foot cabin was reconstructed inside a
new marble-and-granite memorial reached only by climbing
fifty-six steps—one step for each year Lincoln lived. Let's just
call it Lincoln's Symbolic Birthplace. Of course Lincoln lived
there only two years before his dad lost title to the farm. The
family moved 10 miles east to what Lincoln called the "Knob
Creek place," another log cabin.

And sure enough, drive over and you can see yet another
Lincoln log cabin. This one was reconstructed in 1931 on the
original Knob Creek site, using logs that no one has ever
claimed came from the original cabin. No, here they claim some
of the logs came from the Austin Gollaher cabin. There is a
connection: Gollaher once saved young Abe from drowning in
Knob Creek. Let's call it Lincoln's Symbolic Boyhood Home.

The Lincolns left Knob Creek in 1816, crossing the Ohio River
to Indiana at Cloverport. A historical marker denotes the spot.

You can go a little further back in time, Lincoln time, with a
visit to nearby Lincoln Homestead State Park. Here, within
shouting range of a golf course, is where the first Abraham
Lincoln, the future president's grandfather, was killed by Indians. A replica of the family's cabin sits on the site, where tradition has it young Tom grew up. That would be the Symbolic
Ancestral Home. Also nearby, relocated from its original site a
mile away, is a two-story log cabin, the Francis Berry house,
where Nancy Hanks was living when she met Tom Lincoln. It's
not symbolic; it's the real deal.

Abraham Lincoln Birthplace National Historic Site is located 3 miles south of Hodgenville on U.S. 31E. For information call (502) 358–3137. Lincoln's boyhood home, Knob Creek Farm, is located 7 miles northeast of Hodgenville on U.S. 31E. For information call (502) 549–3741. Lincoln Homestead State Park is located 5 miles north of Springfield on KY 438. Call (606) 336–7461.

LINCOLN DAYS

*E*very October, Hodgenville celebrates its Lincoln heritage with Lincoln Days, a festival that includes a rail-splitting competition, a crafts festival, and a parade of Lincoln impersonators. You haven't seen anything until you've see two dozen Lincoln look-alikes (or sort of look-alikes) walking down a city street. For information call (270) 358–8710.

EDGAR CAYCE, "THE SLEEPING PROPHET"
Hopkinsville

You are getting sleepy, very sleepy. When you awake you will be able to place yourself in a trance and predict world events. Does this seem hard to believe? For Edgar Cayce, hypnosis was just the beginning.

Born in Hopkinsville, the "sleeping prophet" began his life as a deeply religious farm boy. As a child, Cayce recalled being able to see ghosts, who would talk to him and help him out. One of the more prominent spirits he claimed to see was that of a gray-haired woman who would come to him when he needed her the most—while studying for school. According to Cayce the apparition instructed him to lie down, and when he awoke he knew all he needed to know to pass his exams. Apparently she wasn't much better at school than Cayce. He ended up dropping out after the eighth grade.

When Cayce was twenty-one years old, he developed a strange condition that paralyzed his vocal cords. Not being able to talk hurt his career as a salesman. Cayce needed help, and he needed it fast. Doctors prescribed remedies that didn't work, so Cayce turned to hypnotist Al Layne. Layne taught Cayce how to place himself under a "healing self-induced trance."

The trance worked. In fact, according to Cayce, it worked too well. While under a trance, Cayce was able to predict the future. He could also diagnose patients' illnesses with just a name and address. On October 9, 1910, the *New York Times* published an article on Cayce's talents, "Illiterate Man Becomes a Doctor When Hypnotized; Strange Power Shown By Edgar Cayce Puzzles Physicians." The article brought Cayce national fame.

Soon Cayce was bombarded with requests for health readings and "life" readings, where he could tell someone who they were in a past life. Cayce also began making grim predictions of the future, all which were recorded and published. Some of the more notable predictions were the rise of Atlantis in 1968 and the second coming of Christ in 1998, which would be immortalized with a shift in the earth's poles and "superquakes." Cayce also saw himself reborn in postapocalypse Nebraska in 2100.

In 1931 Cayce moved to Virginia Beach and formed the Association for Research and Enlightenment (ARE). On New Year's Day, 1945, Cayce became ill and predicted to everyone, from a trance of course, that he would be miraculously cured of his illness. Three days later, Cayce died at the age of sixty-seven.

There's a Cayce display at the Pennyroyal Area Museum, 217 East Ninth Street; (270) 887–4270.

S *TINK* C *AVE*
Horse Cave

Pop quiz: Horse Cave was named "Horse Cave" because: a) A horse powered pumping device was used to remove water from the cave; b) a horse fell over the cliff leading into the cave and died; c) a gang of thieves used the cave to hide the horses they stole from local townspeople; d) it's not called Horse Cave; it's actually called "Stink Cave"; or e) all of the above.

The correct answer: all of the above.

Nestled at the bottom of a sinkhole, Horse Cave has a freshwater river running through the middle of it. Shortly after it was first discovered, locals used the resource for their water supply, using horses to cart numerous pumping devices and pipes to lift the water from the cave to the surface. The cave became a tourist attraction in 1925 when Dr. Harry B. Thomas opened it for tours and social gatherings. At the attraction's peak, groups of socialites would make the trek down steep stairs, over the water, and through the mud to the cave's largest dome, where they held dances during the warm summer months.

Prosperous times were short-lived for Horse Cave, and in 1943 it was closed. For years locals had not only been using the cave's water resources but also polluting it. Area townspeople built their outhouses near sinkholes that led directly to the river flowing inside the cave. The sinkholes, a natural phenomenon in this region, also became the town dump, filled with trash, dead animals, and anything that wouldn't burn. The pollution was so bad that a geologist touring the cave stated that the river was pitch black with feces and waste. As you can imagine, the pollution had a profound effect on the town; a horrendous stench filled the air and was only compounded by the summer heat. Thomas was forced to close the cave—not for a lack of interested people willing to put up with the stench to see it, but because the smell was so bad that people passed out before they could get to the entrance.

In 1970 the government got involved and issued a decree that the townspeople could no longer dump their trash or waste in any area that would affect the cave. It took a while, but in 1983, after being closed for forty years, Horse Cave reopened for business.

While the townspeople still refer to the cave as Horse Cave and the cave does sit in Horse Cave City, if you go there, you won't find it. As part of the restoration efforts and attempt to get the townspeople behind the idea of cleaning up the pollution, a contest was held to rename the cave. It is now Hidden River Cave. However, it still goes by Horse Cave, and Stink Cave, and . . . well, you get the idea. In any case, it's not open to the public.

ONLY KNOWN GUN BATTLE BETWEEN MARTIANS AND KENTUCKIANS

Some say it never happened. Some say it happened but not the way you heard it. Danny McCord isn't sure. "My aunt was a religious woman, and she swore to her dying day that it was aliens," he says.

Something happened on that October night in 1955, and it deeply affected the people of Kelly, Kentucky, a wide place in the road 8 miles north of Hopkinsville. They say that Gaither McGehee, his wife and sons, and a neighbor boy were sitting at the kitchen table that night when they saw a light in the field. Being Kentuckians, they went for their guns and went for the light. They would later claim that they saw little green men emerge from a UFO in the field. The Kentuckians and the aliens exchanged gunfire before the Kentucky boys retreated inside the house. When the sheriff investigated the next day, he found a wooden house pockmarked with square bullet holes. He vowed to newspaper reporters that it had to have been aliens. "These are not drinking people," he pointed out.

When I investigated recently, the fellow who ran the bait shop nearby told me that the sheriff didn't know those people. "They were carnival people." He swore it was just a drunken brawl. How to explain the square bullet holes? "That's from the bullets coming out of the house, not going in." Sad to report, the house was torn down in the seventies.

Aliens or alcohol? You decide.

THE WORLD'S LARGEST APPLE PIE
Liberty

There's nothing more American than apple pie and Big Wheels! For the last full week of September, Casey County kicks off the fall season with the Casey County Apple Festival, held in downtown Liberty. More than 50,000 people attend the event every year, making it one of the largest festivals in the state. A fall festival is common for Kentucky. In fact, most counties have one; some even have an apple festival. But they don't have what Casey County has . . . a 3,500-pound apple pie.

The Casey County Apple Festival is home to the world's largest apple pie. The pie takes three hours to build and ten hours to cook, is 10 feet in diameter and 8 inches deep, and serves 8,500. While most people come to the festival for the pie, there are other things that keep them coming back year after year, including crafts, vendor booths, and a Big Wheels race. Where else are you going to be able to eat a piece of the world's largest apple pie and see grown men compete on Big Wheels?

For information on the festival call (606) 787–6241.

MIKE'S MYSTERY SPOT
Mammoth Cave

"Are you afraid of snakes? That's OK, because there are no snakes at Mike's Mystery House."

Cheesey opening, yes, but this is how the tour of Mike's Mystery House begins. Located just outside Mammoth Cave National Park, Mike's Mystery House is, in fact, no real mystery. For a

*It's no mystery that the entrepreneurial spirit is
alive and well at Mike's Mystery House.*

dollar, visitors can take a tour of a "gravity-defying" area, conveniently located behind Big Mike's Rock and Gift Shop.

Admission to the tour includes one-liner jokes, endless puns
and double entendres, and a maze of black lighting that helps
add to the spooky kitsch of it all. In addition to being one of
the rare places on earth that have gravity-pull centers, Mike's
Mystery House is also one of the world's largest tributes to
Spencer's Gifts stores, a fact that is brought up numerous
times during the journey as you are encouraged to touch the
glow-in-the-dark posters, electric balls, and lava lamps.

Big Mo, the Mystery Beast, welcomes you to Mammoth Cave.

Guests get to feel firsthand the effect of the gravitational pull in the house. You can crawl up a wall, sit in a chair that is placed against the wall midway up, and walk up the wall using some strategically placed steps. As you wind yourself down from the excitement of the "mystery spot," with the aid of some fun-house mirrors, the tour comes to an end. But that's not all! Luckily the tour just happens to end right inside Mike's store, where you can stock up on various souvenirs, cups, shirts, and rocks. There's no admission charge to tour the souvenir shop. But that doesn't mean it won't cost you.

You'll feel the pull at 566 Old Mammoth Cave Road in Cave City; (270) 773–5144.

MOONSHINE CAPITAL OF THE WORLD

Since there's no official government designation for Moonshine Capital of the World, there are a number of claimants to the title:

Climax, Virginia, stages an annual Moonshiners Jamboree. Cosby, Tennessee, in the foothills of the Great Smoky Mountains, also lays claim to the title, as does Rocky Mount, Virginia, which managed to get the New York Times to call it "the moonshine capital of the world." Brasstown, North Carolina, used to claim the title. It now prefers to be called the Opossum Capital of the World.

But if you've ever seen the lay of the land in Land Between the Lakes, you know this is the place. It doesn't get any more remote than this.

In The Antecedents of Southern Organized Crime, Dr. Gary W. Potter of Eastern Kentucky University calls the area a "very important moonshine enclave." He notes that the Golden Pond area between the Cumberland and Tennessee Rivers produced a moonshine whiskey that was highly sought during Prohibition. "In an area with no more than 300 inhabitants, and no airport, it is said that dozens of planes flew in and out on a weekly basis carrying the prized brew to Chicago and New York." The Capone syndicate, Meyer Lansky, Bugsy Siegel, and Owney "the Killer" Madden all looked to Golden Pond for their hooch. Potter says, "Moonshining was so organized and demand so intense that each hollow had as many as fifteen stills operating."

Of course that was a long time ago. But once the Moonshine Capital of the World, always the Moonshine Capital of the World.

WORLD'S STRANGEST BARBECUE SANDWICH
Owensboro

Ask for a barbecue sandwich at any of Owensboro's half-dozen or so barbecue eateries, and you may be surprised. Barbecue in Owensboro isn't pork, as it is in most of America. And it isn't beef, as it is in Texas. It's mutton. Mutton! Sheep meat! And no one in town can tell you for sure why that is.

If you ask "What's for lunch," at Owensboro BBQs,
you're likely to get a reply of "Mutton, honey."

Henry Etta Schauberger and Stan LeMaster, who wrote the definitive history of Owensboro barbecue for the Daviess County Historical Society in 1970, could only conjecture that it was because the area was a major sheep-producing region during the Civil War. But they also note that after the turn of the twentieth century, sheep were getting scarce because of rampaging packs of dogs. Whatever the reason, accept it. And accept mutton. It is, as Andy Griffith used to say, gooooooood—a bit stronger than beef, not as sweet as pork, but tasty—and different.

Owensboro has declared itself the "Barbecue Capital of the World." Just insert "Mutton" before "Barbecue" and you won't get any argument anywhere. Every May they celebrate the fact with the International Bar-B-Q Festival, an event that draws more than 100,000 people to Owensboro's riverfront (it's the Ohio) to watch church cooking teams compete for bragging rights. Tourists benefit as well: Once the judging has concluded, the churches sell that barbecue to anybody with a five-dollar bill and a big appetite.

For more information on the International Bar-B-Q Festival call (270) 926–6938.

WASHINGTON COUNTY SORGHUM AND TOBACCO FESTIVAL AND FAIR
Springfield

It's not an appetizing sounding combination. Not many people would naturally put sorghum and tobacco together, but when both grow in abundance in your town, what else are you going to do? Every year Springfield hosts the Sorghum and Tobacco Festival.

To fully appreciate the festival, you first need to know what sorghum is. Sorghum is a grasslike plant that is ground and the juices extracted to make a molasses-like product.

Held the first week of October, the Sorghum and Tobacco Festival draws a crowd of about 15,000 and even has its own motto: "Always a major success for the whole family." And it is. There is a buffet breakfast every morning so that visitors can sample the rich molasses grown in the fields out back and made next door. After breakfast, you can light up a cigarette and watch molasses being made. As we all know, there's nothing slower than molasses! Maybe you should bring a carton of cigarettes—it's going to be a long festival.

For festival information call (606) 336–3810.

THE TOWN NOBODY WANTS
Static

The town of Static, on the Kentucky-Tennessee border near Dale Hollow Lake, is an orphan, rejected by both states. Kentucky says it's in Tennessee, and Tennessee says it's in Kentucky. Visit and you may decide they're both right. It's nowhere. It definitely lives up to its name; there's not a lot happening.

The major industries in town are selling gasoline and selling lottery tickets. You'll recognize the Kentucky side of town immediately. That's where all the lottery ticket signs are. Before you leave, you should check out an interesting highway sign on TN 111. It directs the traveler to nearby Jamestown— and it points both ways.

To reach Static, go right on U.S. 127 southbound to Jamestown, Tennessee. Go left on U.S. 127 to Jamestown, Kentucky. Then go figure.

JESSE JAMES ROBS BANK; EVERYONE HAPPY

*J*esse James robbed the Southern Bank in Russellville, and they're still proud of the fact today. But James's connection to Kentucky began long before his days of crime. His parents, Robert and Zerelda James, were married in Stamping Ground, Kentucky, and his brother, Frank, was born there. Just before Jesse was born, the family moved to Missouri; shortly thereafter, the father deserted the family and moved west, caught up in the gold rush. He never did find his riches, though. He didn't really have much time to do so. After arriving on the West Coast, Robert James died of food poisoning. Some people speculate that the absence of his father is what led Jesse to a life of crime. Others say that he really didn't commit the crimes attributed to him. Regardless, his legend grew, and the Southern Deposit Bank was just a stopping point for him.

Jesse ran with a gang of bandits, which included his older brother and random criminals who wanted in on easy hits. Jesse was the youngest and least experienced of the group—and some say not the brightest in the pack, either. However, he was the prettiest, and he knew it. Jesse loved to have his picture taken and did so at nearly every stop he and the gang made. It was his good looks that distinguished him from the rest of the group, thus newspapers and people attributed many of the crimes to him alone.

On March 20, 1868, Jesse and his crew entered the Southern Deposit Bank at Sixth and Main Streets in Russellville. Reports at the time said that they walked away with $12,000 to $14,000. However, later reports claimed that Jesse and his brother were not even there. The initial crime report states that five men were involved in the heist. Eyewitnesses were able to describe each man in detail. While the men described did match the descriptions of some of the men known to have run with Jesse and his brother, no one said that the James boys were there. After the reports had been taken, a Detective Blyh came down from Louisville, investigated, and decided that Jesse had not only been there but was in charge of the entire operation.

With the announcement that Jesse James and his gang had robbed their bank, Russellville became a media boomtown, and Jesse would be linked to Kentucky once again. After a fifteen-year crime spree that included an April 1872 bank robbery in Columbia, Kentucky, Jesse James announced his retirement—well, not publicly, but to the boys in his gang. In December 1881 he adopted the alias Tom Howard and rented a home in St. Joseph, Missouri. But retirement only made Jesse a target. Four months later, a man named Bob Ford broke into "Mr. Howard's" home and shot him in the head.

WHERE TWO QUEENS ARE
BETTER THAN ONE
Tompkinsville

A festival with two queens? The annual Watermelon and Barbeque Festival in Tompkinsville celebrates the area's unique
blend of barbeque and watermelons. Why? Because you have to
have dessert.

The festival began in 1980 and draws a crowd of about
7,000. They have cakewalks, crafts, and all the usual things
that go with festivals. However, they also have the world's
largest watermelon auction. People flock to bid on the season's
latest crop of the summer fruit. As an added bonus, they also
throw in entertainment for the whole family with a tractor
pull, antique car show, and an old-fashioned "pickin' and
singin'" contest.

Each year a Watermelon queen and a Barbeque queen are
crowned, and the two queens rule this festival with equal
responsibilities.

If the thought of two queens isn't enough to get your attention, this will: There's also the Privy Prix, an Outhouse Race—
as in outhouses on wheels being raced down the main street.
Most people think it's the other way around: Race to the outhouse. It usually is.

For more information call (502) 487–5504.

QUINTESSENTIAL KENTUCKIANS
Pee Wee Reese, the Boy of Summer

*H*e was a Hall of Fame shortstop for the Brooklyn Dodgers—the Southerner who put his arm around Jackie Robinson early in Robinson's first season, breaking baseball's color line and signaling that baseball was willing to accept black players. But for an entire generation of baseball fans, Reese was better known as Dizzy Dean's sidekick on CBS-TV's Game of the Week.

Reese, who was born in tiny Ekron, Kentucky, and grew up in Louisville, captained the Dodgers during their glory years in the fifties. After his retirement from baseball in 1958, CBS hired Reese to team with the outrageous Dizzy Dean on its baseball telecasts.

Dean—ol' Diz, he called himself—was famous for saying and doing anything that came to his mind. (He once left the booth, telling Reese on the air, "Going to get a steak sandwich. Be back in twenty, thirty minutes.") And during lulls in the action, Dean was apt to break into an off-key rendition of "Wabash Cannonball."

Reese tried to keep the audience focused on the field, but with ol' Diz that was almost impossible. Their most famous play-by-play came during a boring game at Yankee Stadium. As the camera panned the right-field bleachers, desperate to find any action, it paused briefly on an amorous couple who didn't even know there was a ball game going on.

Diz perked up. "Yessir, Pee Wee, there's a young couple that's having a good time at the game. Appears to me he's kissing her on the strikes . . . and she's kissing him on the balls."

The legend of that famous afternoon has grown and grown over the years. Reese said in a 1991 interview with the author that he had had literally thousands of people stop him in airports over the years to tell him they were watching that afternoon. At first he protested, but after a few hundred, he quit arguing. But he insisted, "It never happened. That was an old joke when I broke into baseball." It makes for a great Diz-and-Pee Wee story—even if it never really happened.

THE JACKSON PURCHASE

THE JACKSON PURCHASE

Many people wonder why the western tip of Kentucky—an islandlike land mass bounded by the Kentucky, Ohio, and Mississippi Rivers—is called the Jackson Purchase. It's very simple: Andrew Jackson bought it.

The Purchase, as locals call it, wasn't added to the Kentucky map until more than two decades after statehood. That's when a commission headed by General Jackson, fresh off his triumphs in the War of 1812, negotiated a deal with the local Chickasaw Indians. Actually they could have called it the Shelby Purchase; the deal was brokered jointly by Jackson and former Kentucky Governor Isaac Shelby, and in all the documents Shelby's name is above Jackson's.

The treaty, signed on October 19, 1818, in northwestern Mississippi, gave the fledgling U.S. government title to some 4,600 square miles of land that would be divvied up between Kentucky and Tennessee. In return the Chickasaw would be paid $300,000—$20,000 a year for fifteen years.

At least that's the way the schoolbooks tell it. That's because the schoolbooks didn't have all the facts. It seems that not all the Chickasaws wanted to sell their tribal land. In fact a lot of them didn't, and they threatened anyone who negotiated a treaty with the government. But Jackson and Shelby, by using, um, let's call it "backdoor financing," induced Chief Levi Colbert to sign over all the Chickasaw land in Kentucky and Tennessee. *The Journal on Negotiations of the Chickasaw Treaty of 1818*, kept by the commission, puts it this way: "The Commissioners have been able to ascertain from the transactions of this week that an appeal becomes absolutely necessary to the avarice of the Chiefs."

To protect the tribesmen who signed the deal—and took the bribes—from retribution, Jackson ordered the treaty minutes be kept secret. And they were, for more than one hundred years. Those Chickasaw who couldn't be bribed were merely threatened. From the "secret" journal, this note: "General Jackson also told you that if you refuse to sell your claim that your white brothers would move on this land which is granted to them, and then your nation would have to apply to Congress for compensation, for if you refuse the good intentions of your father the President you cannot look to him for redress."

That $300,000 might not sound like much, but the land Jackson was buying wasn't much either; it was mostly uninhabited and, at the time, pretty uninhabitable. Still, it was a bargain at what would be a little over three million in today's dollars.

BIG SINGING DAY
Benton

In 1835 almost no one in America could read music. Heck, almost no one in America could read anything. So singing teacher William Walker devised a way to solve that: what he called "shaped notes," four shapes that told singers what notes to sing. He published a hymnal using his patented note system, *The Southern Harmony and Musical Companion: Containing a Choice Collection of Tunes, Hymns, Psalms, Odes, and Anthems; Selected from the Most Eminent Authors in the United States: Together with Nearly One Hundred New Tunes Which Have Never Before Been Published; Suited to Most of the Metres Contained in Watts's Hymns and Psalms, Mercer's Cluster, Dossey's Choice, Dover Selection, Methodist Hymn Book, and Baptist Harmony.* And despite the marathon title, it was a huge success.

Jump ahead to 1884. James R. Lemon, a newspaper publisher in Benton, organizes a Big Singing—an all-day community festival and homecoming with singing, singing, and more singing.

Jump ahead to today. The Big Singing is now the oldest indigenous music festival in the United States. It doesn't draw the crowds it once did when special trains were chartered to bring people from all over the South. But 10,000 people is still quite a sight—and sound.

Big Singing Day is held each May on the grounds of the Marshall County Courthouse in Benton. For details call the Marshall County Chamber of Commerce at (270) 527-7665.

CASEY JONES AND THE CANNONBALL EXPRESS

*T*he world has Sim Webb to thank for perpetuating the legend of Casey Jones. Webb rode with Jones as the train fireman the infamous night of the "Cannonball Express."

John Luther "Casey" Jones's legend begins in Cayce, Kentucky, the town that gave him his nickname. Jones became enamored with trains and railroads at an early age. When he was fifteen years old, Jones moved to Columbus, Kentucky, to work at the north terminal of the Mobile and Ohio (M&O) Railroad as a telegrapher. Soon he was promoted to brakeman on runs from Columbus to Jackson, Tennessee. In 1888 Jones left M&O and joined the Illinois Central Railroad, settling down with his wife in Jackson.

Life was good for Jones. In 1890 he was promoted to engineer and made runs from Jackson to Water Valley, Mississippi. In 1900 he was assigned to the Cannonball Express with runs from Memphis to Canton, Mississippi. The Cannonball Express was an assignment most engineers refused due to the high speeds and danger, but Jones loved his new duty.

At 3:52 A.M. on April 30, 1900, Jones' was heading for Canton when three trains met at an intersection in Vaughan, Mississippi. This was not uncommon, and the trains attempted a "saw-by" that would have allowed Jones's express train to pass through. However, an air hose on one of the trains broke and left four cars stranded on the mainline. Jones didn't see the cars until it was too late. He yelled at Webb to jump just before the trains collided. Casey stayed on trying to slow the train down as much as possible to save his passengers. He did—but he couldn't save himself. And thus was born the legend "The Ballad of Casey Jones."

Webb passed the story of Casey Jones onto Wallace Saunders, who worked in the engine shop with the two, and Saunders wrote the song that told "the story about a brave engineer." The song was popularized by a couple of vaudeville performers, Siebert and Newton, who—legend has it—bought the song from Saunders for a pint of whiskey. Now there's the real legend of Casey Jones.

TATER DAYS
Benton

Kentucky has festivals for fruit, farm animals, and music. The state would not be complete without a festival honoring a side dish of some kind. Leave it to Benton to come to the rescue with the world's only—as far as we know—salute to the sweet potato.

Benton is home of the Tater Day Festival—Tater Days, as it is known—a three-day event held on the weekend before the first Monday in April, honoring the sweet potato.

This form of tuber was all the rage back in 1843 during court days, bringing in high bidding and trading values. Sweet potatoes grow well in Kentucky's hot, humid summer weather, making the tuber an easy cash crop.

To honor the spud there is a parade, carnival, and fiddling contest, as well as baking and canning contests. How many ways can you fix a sweet potato? At least enough to fill judging for three days.

For more information call (270) 527-3767.

KENTUCKY IN MISSOURI—WHERE THE MISSISSIPPI CHANGED COURSE
Columbus

Kentuckians in the Mississippi River town of Columbus were as happy as a bug in a rug in 1811. Then on December 16 a natural disaster struck that would shake their world—literally. A massive earthquake hit about 25 miles away in New Madrid, Missouri. That quake remains the most severe recorded earthquake to hit the continental United States. New Madrid, a town of 400 on the banks of the Mississippi, was totally destroyed. Three more smaller—but not much—quakes happened over the next seven weeks. This seismic activity, now referred to as the Great New Madrid Earthquake of 1811–1812, caused the Mississippi River to change course. Some locals claimed it even flowed backward for a few days.

When the mighty Mississippi shifted its shores, it left a part of what was then Livingston (now Hickman) County hanging, literally, pinched off and shoved into Missouri. Over time Missourians noticed that a large chunk of Kentucky was on their side of the river, and in time they decided to stake a claim to it. The case wound up in the United States Supreme Court, where in 1871 the justices ruled that despite its new location on the Missouri side of the Mississippi, the land would remain part of Kentucky.

Kentucky Highway 58 takes you across the mighty Mississippi. Turn left on the first road in Missouri, Wolf Island Road, and you can drive into the once disputed chunk of land.

WORLD'S LARGEST ONE-DAY PICNIC
Fancy Farm

They say you can't even get elected dogcatcher in Kentucky if you don't speak at the annual Fancy Farm Picnic. That's what draws crowds of 15,000 and more—that and the barbecue. Cooks roast up more than nine tons of pork and mutton—a ton more than they cooked in 1984, the year the Guinness World Record people bestowed on Fancy Farm the title of World's Largest One-Day Picnic.

The Fancy Farm Picnic has been a must for political candidates of all stripes since before the Civil War. The fighting caused the event to be halted for a time, but it picked back up in 1880 and has been an annual event, the unofficial kickoff of the fall campaign, ever since.

Any candidate—local, state, or national—can speak, as long as he or she follows the rules: No speaking before 2:00 P.M. That gives everyone a chance to eat. And no speaking after 4:00 P.M. That gives everyone a chance to eat again. Oh, yeah, and you have to speak next to the aptly named lyin' tree, a dead oak that got its name from the free flow of campaign promises beneath its branches. The tree was felled in 1974 by what is known around here as "a nonpartisan bolt of lightning."

The Fancy Farm Picnic is held the first Saturday in August at St. Jerome Church on Kentucky Highway 339 in Fancy Farm. For more information call St. Jerome Church at (270) 623–8181 or contact the Mayfield-Graves County Chamber of Commerce at (270) 247–6101.

HAZEL DAY CELEBRATION
Hazel

Hazel is the antiques capital of western Kentucky. So let's have a party!

Held on the first Saturday in October, the Hazel Day Celebration—not a festival, mind you—celebrates everything old: old cars, old games, old people. There is an old-fashioned cakewalk, and a not-so-old-fashioned washer-pitching contest. No, not your GE model, the real old-fashioned washer things. Hearts begin to palpitate and beat just a little faster when the checkers tournament closes out the celebration.

The celebration has been going strong since 1990, with no signs of getting old yet. Sorry for that.

For more information on the Hazel Day Celebration call (270) 492–8796.

WORLD'S LARGEST BANANA PUDDING

*F*ulton, Kentucky, was the reigning banana capital of the world until 1992—and I bet you thought it was South America! More than 70 percent of the world's banana shipments were sent through the tiny town. Bananas were loaded into refrigerator cars, "ice reefers" they were called, in New Orleans and shipped north by rail. The ice only lasted to Fulton, so the town became a stopping-off point where all the trains would stock up with a fresh supply of block ice to prevent the bananas from spoiling. Some of the trains were a mile long with banana cars.

Wanting to celebrate their claim to fame, Fulton began the International Banana Festival in 1962. And what's a festival without a gimmick? Fulton's festival had several. First there was the banana hat contest, then the parade of fruit. And finally there was the world's largest banana pudding. Clearly the highlight of the festival, the pudding weighed more than a ton and served thousands.

But, alas, the banana industry isn't what it used to be, and Fulton lost its distinction as the Banana Capital—and its festival. After a thirty-year run, the International Banana Festival is no more. Now you have to go to a local restaurant if you want banana pudding.

THE PROCESSION THAT NEVER MOVES
Mayfield

The world's slowest moving procession is located in Mayfield. Why is it so slow? Because it's a procession of statues—Giant cement statues of the Wooldridge family, complete with lifelike dogs.

Dubbed "the strange procession that never moves," it features eighteen statues and adorns the entryway to the tomb of Colonel Henry Wooldridge, who was a horse trader. When he died in 1899 he commanded in his will that life-size replicas of his family be created and surround his tomb. The images of his aunts, sisters, uncles, parents, grandparents, and even the family dogs, Tow Head and Bob, are forever carved in stone for the world to see.

You've probably seen the monuments before. They made an appearance in the 1989 Bruce Willis movie *In Country,* which was filmed in these parts.

The Colonel is the only person actually entombed there. Unfortunately for the tourist, there's a fence surrounding the monument, thwarting would-be vandals—and would-be photographers.

The statues and procession can be found at Maplewood Cemetery on North Sixth Street in Mayfield. (There is no phone.)

BERT & BUD'S DEAD BUSINESS
Murray

Say you weren't fortunate enough to have your leg blown off at the Battle of Perryville and die a horrible death from gangrene. Say you were just a run-of-the-mill Civil War reenactor who left this world by natural causes. That doesn't mean you can't ship out in Civil War style. You can. Just contact Bert & Bud, or have your nearest survivor do it for you.

Bert & Bud make caskets. But not just any caskets. Albert "Bert" Sperath and Roy "Bud" Davis make custom caskets. They say your casket is your final opportunity to make a profound statement about your life—as their ads promise, "To say, 'This is how I want to be remembered.'"

*If you're game, you can take a trip down the River Styx
in one of Bert & Bud's custom coffins.*

You can be remembered in a simple wooden coffin or something a little more elaborate, a little more personal. After all,
who wants to make that final journey in an assembly-line
casket? And if you enjoyed Civil War reenacting in life, why
not enjoy it in death, too, with a Civil War–era casket.

Bert & Bud promise that coffins are "built one at a time to
the measurements, specifications, and tastes of each customer."
You may remember the slogan from your high-school year-
book. On the ad for the local funeral home, some funnyman
had added: "We're the last to let you down." That's Bert & Bud.

For more information call Bert & Bud at (270) 753–9279.

QUINTESSENTIAL KENTUCKIANS
Happy Chandler, Happy Man

*H*is name was Albert Benjamin, but nobody called him that. Even his wife called him Happy. It was a nickname he acquired during the twenties as an ever-smiling student athlete at Transylvania College in Lexington.

Happy was a Harvard-educated lawyer, but you would never have known it. How many Harvard lawyers sing to their constituents? That's what Happy did when he first ran for Kentucky governor in 1935. He would later brag that he ran his campaign "with a seventy-five dollar sound truck and a pitcher of ice water." During the campaign he traveled to every county in the state, speaking five times each day, and closing each rally by singing college songs, hymns and, of course, the state song, "My Old Kentucky Home."

He won, serving as governor from 1935 to 1939. Near the end of Happy's term the state's senior U.S. senator M. M. Logan, died. The opportunistic Chandler, who always seemed to be more interested in his next job, resigned his post as governor, and his successor, Lieutenant Governor Keen Johnson, succeeded him and appointed him to the senate job.

While in Washington, Happy became a fan of the Washington Senators baseball club, attending games when he should perhaps have been in the Senate chambers. He became friends with many baseball owners, and in 1945 he resigned his Senate seat to succeed Judge Kenesaw Mountain Landis as baseball's second commissioner.

It was during his tenure that Jackie Robinson broke baseball's color line, an historic event that Happy claimed to have championed. His detractors said that he fought it until it happened and then grabbed the credit. He resigned in 1951 after the baseball team owners refused to extend his contract and returned to Kentucky to run for governor again. He was elected and served from 1955 to 1959. A state law prevented him from succeeding himself. He ran again in '63, '67, and '71, but voters had tired of his act.

In his last years he became famous for singing "My Old Kentucky Home" at University of Kentucky home basketball games and for making outrageous comments at U.K. board of trustees meetings.

When Happy resigned as baseball commissioner in 1951, the publisher of The Sporting News, J. G. Taylor Spink, had this telling assessment: "Happy insisted on being himself." Happy Chandler was elected to baseball's Hall of Fame in 1982; he died in 1991.

MARCONI, SCHMONI—
RADIO WAS BORN HERE
Murray

Poor Nathan Stubblefield. He invented radio and didn't even get a lousy T-shirt, much less any mention in the history books. Of course it didn't help any that Nathan was secretive, suspicious, and stubborn. Nor did it help that he died in 1929 in his shack of starvation, leading people to think of him less as a genius than as a mad genius.

It all dates to 1892, when Stubblefield demonstrated his Stubblefield's Black Box to a friend named Rainey T. Wells. He handed Wells one black box and told him to walk away. When Wells got a couple of hundred yards down the path, he heard a distinct noise coming from his box. "Hello, Rainey," the voice said. Let's let Rainey pick up the story. "I jumped a foot and said to myself, *This fellow is fooling me. He has wires some-place.*" Rainey kept moving, but the voice kept following. "All the while he kept talking to me . . . but there were no wires, I tell you."

It would be ten years before Stubblefield was ready for a public demonstration, and he chose the steps of the Calloway County Courthouse. He set up one box on the steps and directed his son, Bernard, to set up a second box some 200 feet away. He and Bernard then began conducting a conversation as if they were standing next to each other, much to the astonishment of a large throng gathered around. He later demonstrated the device at a distance of 1 mile for an amazed *St. Louis Post-Dispatch* reporter, who listened as Bernard played the harmonica and sang.

Stubblefield made an attempt at marketing his invention, but the company he threw in with, the Philadelphia-based Wireless

Telephone Company of America, turned out to be a scam set up for the purpose of selling stock, not developing a product. Bitter, Stubblefield retired to his shack and wasn't heard from again until his body was found by a neighbor.

There is much debate about what Stubblefield actually invented. A modern analysis of his patents and the historical record don't fully support a claim as the Father of Radio. But almost no one disputes that son Bernard was the first person to broadcast music to an audience, even if it was an audience of one, the St. Louis reporter.

A stone memorial on the campus of Murray State College commemorates his legend. "Here, in 1902, Nathan Stubblefield (1860–1928), inventor of radio, broadcast and received human voice by wireless."

WORKING STIFF—KENTUCKY'S MUMMY
Paducah

Speedy Atkins was just a working stiff, a messenger in a tobacco company, when he went fishing on that fateful day in 1928. He fell asleep on the bank, tumbled into the Ohio River, and drowned.

When authorities could find no next of kin to the lifelong bachelor, they turned his body over to funeral home attendant A. Z. Hamock, who worked at Watkins Undertaking Parlor, the city's only African-American funeral home, for a pauper's burial. But Hamock decided instead to experiment with an embalming fluid he had been developing. The result turned Speedy into something that looked like a wooden statue.

Hamock was so taken with the result he decided that rather than bury Speedy, he would put him on display in the funeral home. And that's where Speedy resided for almost three-quarters of a century. In death the anonymous messenger became famous, appearing on a number of national TV shows, including *That's Incredible, Ripley's Believe It or Not,* and *A Current Affair.*

Hamock's widow Velma, decided she was going to bury old Speedy in 1991 on her late husband's one-hundredth birthday, but you know how things are. She didn't get around to it until May 1994. And that's where Speedy is today.

Speedy's grave is in the Maplelawn Cemetery, 1335 North Thirteenth Street. For information call (270) 442–2538.

HOME OF THE ATOMIC BOMB

*P*erhaps you thought it was Los Alamos—or Oak Ridge. Ah, it's all in the wording: not "Birthplace of," "Home of."

The atomic bomb wasn't invented in Paducah. But since 1952 Paducah has been home to an operating uranium-enrichment facility. And since 2001 it has been home to the only operating uranium enrichment facility in the United States. What does that mean? It means that if you are afraid of acquiring an eerie green glow, you might not want to move here. Not that any locals have a green glow, but this is the place where radioactive uranium is enriched so that it can fuel, oh, a bomb. They don't do that anymore and haven't produced any bomb-grade enriched uranium since 1962. We have treaties and all. Now Paducah produces fuel for nuclear power plants.

Why Paducah? Some think it might have something to do with the fact that when the contract was awarded in 1950, the vice president of the U-S-of-A was none other than Alben Barkley, a native of nearby Graves county who had once practiced law in Paducah.

The Paducah Gaseous Diffusion Plant is located some 10 miles west of town near the Ohio River in McCracken County. Yes, there's a big fence.

QUINTESSENTIAL KENTUCKIANS
Irvin S. Cobb

*K*entucky humorist Irvin Cobb, whose glory years on the literary scene were the first third of the twentieth century, was a writer and storyteller known the world over for his sly wit and good Kentucky sense. The short, portly Cobb, with his ever-present cigar, was a fixture on the New York literary scene. He wrote sixty books and more than 300 short stories, sixteen of which were turned into films, including the 1933 Cary Grant film Woman Accused, the 1934 Will Rogers comedy Judge Priest, and the 1953 John Ford film The Sun Shines Bright. His success made him the highest paid writer of his day, favorably compared with Mark Twain and Edgar Allen Poe.

He once quipped, "A good storyteller is a person who has a good memory and hopes other people haven't." Commenting on the nation's capital, he noted, "Washington is a good place to go crazy because it will not be noticed." His most prescient quote was this one: "If writers were good businessmen, they'd have too much sense to be writers."

But times, and tastes in humor, change; today his books are out of print and his words are mostly found in a few works of familiar quotes. Even in his hometown of Paducah people know him, if at all, as the namesake for the landmark Hotel Irvin S. Cobb, now the Irvin Cobb Apartments, or the local highway, Irvin Cobb Drive.

MUSEUM OF THE AMERICAN QUILTER'S SOCIETY
Paducah

I n Kentucky quilts are quilts; they are handmade blankets that folks use to keep themselves warm. But in other parts of the country, quilts are collectibles, a form of folk art. We didn't realize that for a long time. So quilt "dealers" were coming into the state, buying up our quilts, carting them off, and selling them for three, four, ten times what they bring here.

We woke up to that fact in the eighties and began treating quilts for what they are: gorgeous examples of handwork. And thus in 1991 was born the Museum of the American Quilter's Society, a place to house a representative collection while photographing and documenting many others. It's the largest museum of its kind in the world. Why Paducah? Because the founders of the American Quilter's Society, Meredith and Bill Schroeder, live here.

The permanent collection at the museum features quilts from all over, not just Kentucky. If you're lucky enough to be in the area in late April, you can enjoy the annual quilt show; more than 400 quilts are on display, competing for $80,000 in prizes.

Quilts . . . they're not just for bedtime anymore.

The museum is at 215 Jefferson Street; (502) 442–8856. Except for holidays, it's open year-round Monday through Saturday 10:00 A.M. to 5:00 P.M., and on Sunday afternoon from 1:00 to 5:00 P.M., April through October. Admission is free.

Quilts R Us. Quilts of all sizes and shapes are on display at the Museum of the American Quilter's Society.

LADY SELLS THE BOOZE

*T*he dirty looking fellows who knocked at Lucille Edwards's door in 2001 wanted to buy some whiskey. Without even asking for ID the Paducah woman retrieved the liquor, took their money, and was heading back to washing dishes. That's when the thirsty souls revealed their true identities. They were undercover McCracken County Sheriff's deputies—and Miss Lucille was under arrest for "bootlegging."

Edwards later pleaded guilty to the charges and was fined $500 and sentenced to 120 days of home incarceration, not a bad deal for a bootlegger who sold whiskey out the back door of her house. It was Edwards's second offense, but the judge had mercy after her lawyer explained that she was frail. "She never leaves the home anyway," he told the judge. The judge also considered another factor in Edwards's story: She was eighty-two years old and a great-grandmother!

M O N K E Y   M A N
P a d u c a h

You've heard of the infamous Scopes Monkey Trial. It was held in Dayton, Tennessee, in 1925 as a challenge to our sister state's law against teaching evolution. But did you know who the Scopes of the Scopes Monkey Trial was? He was Kentucky native John Thomas Scopes, a substitute teacher who was born in Paducah and graduated from the University of Kentucky in Lexington.

Scopes was a twenty-four-year-old football coach and science teacher when he happened to stop by Robinson's Drug Store in Dayton one May morning in 1925. One of the regulars at the store, George Rappelyea, was reading a *Chattanooga Daily Times* story about Tennessee's new law, the Butler Act, which forbade the teaching of evolution in public schools. The story noted that the American Civil Liberties Union was looking to fund a challenge to the law. Rappelyea thought that just might be what sleepy little Dayton needed—a big show trial that would bring attention, and tourists, to town.

Rappelyea summoned Scopes over. Under questioning, the young Kentuckian admitted that he had taught biology for only two weeks, filling in for the ailing regular teacher. He wasn't even sure what he had covered in those ten days. "We reviewed for final exams, as best I remember."

That was good enough for Rappelyea. And thus was born the most famous trial of the twentieth century with, as its defendant, poor John Scopes, who in all likelihood never taught a single sentence of evolutionary biology.

John Scopes died in 1970 at age seventy and is buried in Section 7, Lot #104 of the Oak Grove Cemetery in Paducah. The cemetery is at 1613 Park Avenue. For information call (270) 444–8532. While you are visiting Oak Grove, you might search out the headstone for Dollie the mule. That's right, a mule in a people cemetery. Dollie was interred in Oak Grove in 1897 after sixteen years of pulling the local fire wagon.

ROAD MAP TO HEAVEN
Tri City

Want to know how to get to heaven? Lesley Murdock can tell you. Even though he died in 1979, Murdock is still offering a road map at his mausoleum.

Murdock, who founded Paradise Friendly Home, the only orphanage in Graves County, specified that his interment site include his instructions—heavy on scripture from the Gospel of John—detailing the road to grace. Murdock and his wife are the only ones buried at the site.

There used to be letters atop the mausoleum that spelled out STOP AND SEE A ROADMAP TO HEAVEN. That's been removed. But there is a plaque that reads ROADMAP TO HEAVEN—WHAT MUST I DO TO BE SAVED? It provides a six-step answer—but if I include that here, then there's no point in visiting the gravesite.

Tri-City is at the intersection of KY 94 and KY 97.

KY-1

KENTUCKY, THE LICENSE PLATE STATE

*O*ur plates read simply BLUEGRASS STATE, despite the fact that no one outside Kentucky has any idea what bluegrass is, much less that it isn't blue. We could put a lot of different slogans on our license plates, because Kentucky truly is the Land of Curiosities. Here are just a few:

THE POST OFFICE STATE—*Kentucky has more post offices per capita than any other state.*

IF YOU CAN READ THIS BUMPER STICKER YOU AREN'T FROM KENTUCKY—*Kentucky has the lowest percentage of adults age twenty-five and over without a high school diploma.*

GREATER KENTUCKY—*Kentucky claims that its border extends all the way to the Indiana shoreline of the Ohio River and has made threats to close down Indiana's casino boats.*

THE GAME SHOW STATE—*Famous game show hosts Jack Narz, Chuck Woolery, and Tom Kennedy are all from Kentucky.*

GATEWAY TO THE WILD WILD WEST—*Judge Roy Bean, Jim Bowie, and Kit Carson were all born in Kentucky*

THE GOVERNOR STATE—*More than a hundred native Kentuckians have been elected governors of other states.*

THE VOLUNTEER STATE—*They call Tennessee the Volunteer State, but in the War of 1812 more than half of all Americans killed in action were Kentuckians.*

Incidentally, all our license plates are manufactured at the Kentucky State Reformatory in LaGrange. They cost about $1.45 each to make.

FROM FUTURE CITY TO RABBIT HASH—

Weird-Named Kentucky Towns

*W*hen out-of-staters ask where Paducah is, locals have a little joke. They say, "It's halfway between Monkeys Eyebrow and Possum Trot." And it is. Monkeys Eyebrow is a defunct community in Ballard County, west of Paducah, and Possum Trot is a dot on the map in Marshall County, to the east. Also nearby are Fancy Farm, in Graves County, and the town of Oscar in Ballard County.

In Kentucky we love giving our towns names that will cause a stranger to bolt upright in surprise . . . or delight. Take Rabbit Hash. It's nothing more than a general store in Boone County on Kentucky Highway 536 just southwest from Cincinnati. The name supposedly derives from the recipe that helped a group of folks survive a particularly harsh flood in 1816. *(The store is at 10021 Lower River Road; 859–586–7744.)*

Future City, near Kevil in Ballard County, supposedly got its name from the developer who was going to build a town, put up the sign—FUTURE CITY—but never got around to building anything. Then there's 88, Kentucky, in Barren County (on KY 90, 7 miles south of Glasgow), which supposedly got its name because one of the founders had 88 cents in his pocket when they were trying to pick a name. At least that's one story. Robert M. Rennick, who traced the names of hundreds of our towns for his 1984 book, Kentucky Place Names, offers a different one: The local postmaster had such poor handwriting that he picked the name because he was sure everyone could read his rendering of those two numerals.

Mud Lick doesn't sound too strange. A bit nasty, but not strange. Maybe that explains why there are nine towns with that name in Kentucky: in Anderson, Elliott, Greenup, Knox, Lewis, Robertson, Russell, Perry and Pike Counties. What does sound disgusting is Paint Lick, a town on KY 52 in Garrard County. Turns out it's not so bad: It was a salt lick marked for prime hunting by Indians, who painted nearby rocks to mark the spot.

There are two Lamb's, one in Kenton County and another in Monroe County. There's no explanation for the town of Typo in Perry County. But you could make up a good story. Bush, Kentucky, in the mountains of Laurel County, was named for George Bush—just not the one you think. The original George Bush founded the town in 1840 when he opened a post office in the general store. The town's original name was Bush's Store. And when the first President Bush campaigned there in 1988, the headline read BUSH RETURNS TO BUSH.

Other curious town names in Kentucky:

Black Gnat, *Taylor County*	Quality, *Butler County*
Black Snake, *Bell County*	Subtle, *Metcalfe County*
Co-operative, *McCreary County*	Susie, *Wayne County*
Crummies, *Harlan County*	Whoopee Hill, *Ohio County*
Hi Hat, *Floyd County*	Wild Cat, *Clay County*

Most everyone's favorite Kentucky town name is Bugtussle, on KY 87 south of Tompkinsville in Monroe County, near the Tennessee border. Fans of The Beverly Hillbillies *may recall that the Clampetts were from Bugtussle, albeit Bugtussle, Tennessee.*

The name, long a synonym for a backwater town, conjures up images of a couple of cockroaches going at it in a wrestling ring. Rennick found a source that claimed the name came from the time of traveling wheat thrashers, who stayed so long sleeping in beds of hay that the bedbugs got huge and began tussling in the bed.

So what about Monkeys Eyebrow and Possum Trot?

Monkeys Eyebrow, which is spelled without the apostrophe, is no more. It was founded at the beginning of the twentieth century by a couple of brothers, John and Dodge Ray, who opened a store on Sand Ridge, some 15 miles west of Wickliffe. The community never had a post office, so it never really mattered where the name came from. But there are numerous tales, most of which have to do with a topographical feature that resembles a monkey's eyebrow. The least likely, but most interesting, was recorded by a WPA researcher, who heard that an ornery local claimed his neighbors in the area "belong to the monkey class."

To see where Monkeys Eyebrow used to be, take KY 473 from Bandana through Ogden. Monkeys Eyebrow once was shortly before the junction with KY 1105.

Possum Trot supposedly got its name when U.S. 62 was under construction in the early years of the twentieth century. After a morning of fruitless hunting, one local told his companion that if they didn't get a possum soon, the possums were going to trot across the road and escape.

Possum Trot is at the intersection of U.S 62 and KY 1610.

NORTHERN KENTUCKY

NORTHERN KENTUCKY

Northern Kentucky is almost indistinguishable from southern Ohio, thanks to their shared cultural center, Cincinnati. But there is a difference. The Cincinnati side is known for its conservatism. Mark Twain once said, "When the end of the world comes, I want to be in Cincinnati—it is always ten years behind the times."

While the north side of the Ohio River, southern Ohio, has given us such wholesome icons as Doris Day and Roy Rogers, the south side, that would be northern Kentucky, is where porn magnate Larry Flynt was born and a pre–tabloid TV Jerry Springer was involved in a sex scandal (he paid a prostitute with a check). It's a little rougher trade on this side of the bridge.

KENTUCKY BIGFOOT
Bedford

Owen Powell was the first person to report it. The creature, more than 6 feet tall and covered with pitch-black hair—"not quite a dog, a panther, or a bear"—was in his hog pen. He sent his dogs after it: not just any old porch dogs, but a German shepherd and a collie. The beast beat them back, sending them whimpering to their master.

Is that the shadow of Bigfoot up there on the ridge?

It was June 3, 1962, and soon Trimble County Sheriff Clem Curtis began receiving other reports of this "Thing," as the locals called it. It was agitating the hogs and stirring up the dogs. Reports continued to trickle in that week of strange animal deaths. There were numerous other spottings. Then, on June 13, a footprint the size of a human hand with four stubby toes was found.

Hanover College zoologist Dr. J. Daniel Webster thought that it was a dog's print but agreed that no dog could create the havoc this "Thing" was wreaking, climbing in barn windows and doing unspeakable things to calves and heifers.

The sheriff's department put on an all-out man, er, beasthunt on June 18, 1962, but found neither hide nor hair of the beast. The Thing was never spotted again. Four decades later they still argue in Trimble County about what this mysterious creature was. Was it a dog—or was it really Bigfoot?

Most of the spottings were on Kidwell Road. The Cliffs, where much of the beasthunt focused, is 1 mile below Hanover, Indiana, on the Kentucky side of the Ohio River.

FORGOTTEN FOURTH—TINKER TO EVERS TO CHANCE TO . . .
Belleview

It is the most famous infield in baseball history, immortalized by Franklin P. Adams in a bit of doggerel he published in the *New York World* in 1910:

These are the saddest of possible words,
Tinker-to-Evers-to-Chance.
Trio of Bear Cubs fleeter than birds,
Tinker-to-Evers-to-Chance.

Joe Tinker, Johnny Evers, and Frank Chance, were, respectively, the shortstop, second baseman, and first baseman of the Chicago Cubs. You don't have to be a student of baseball to recognize that something—or someone—is missing: Harry Steinfeldt. Good old Harry was the third baseman for those great Cubs teams but was sadly neglected by Adams in his famous poem and ended up the answer to a trivia question: Who was the "other" infielder in the Cubs' famous Tinker-to-Evers-to-Chance infield of the early 1900s?

Steinfeldt was every bit the player that Tinker, Evers, and Chance were. In 1906, the year the Cubs set a major league record by winning 116 games, he led the National League in hits and RBIs and was the top-fielding third baseman. Tinker led shortstops in fielding that season; neither Chance nor Evers led at their positions. Steinfeldt's bad luck was that he wasn't part of the Cubs' respected double-play combination.

Right after Adams's poem was published, Steinfeldt had his worst season ever. Whether it had anything to do with being neglected in the poem, we will never know. But it began a downward spiral that culminated on August 17, 1914, when he was killed in a bar fight in Belleview, just three years after retiring at the age of thirty-seven.

GATHERING OF THE CLANS
Carrollton

Is your last name McTavish? Or McCoy or MacVicar or any of the hundreds of other Scottish surnames that populate the phonebooks? Then you may want to rearrange your vacation schedule and meet up with some of your long-lost relatives in a most unlikely place: Kentucky.

*Real men don't wear pants. Men in skirts, er, kilts, gather
at the Scottish Festival.*

Kentucky is not known for its Scottish population; German
and Irish, yes, but not Scottish. Louisville has its Germantown
and was home for many years to the *Irish-American* newspaper. But we have our Scottish clans, too, so to speak. And every
May they gather at General Butler State Resort Park in Carrollton for the Kentucky Scottish Weekend: two days of Scottish
games, good eats, and great fun.

The big crowds assemble for the games. These are not your
ordinary Olympic events. These are brute strength games, like
the 22-pound hammer throw, the 56-pound weight toss, and
the most challenging of all, the caber toss, which involves
hoisting a 175-pound tree trunk. On Saturday you can watch
the pros, then on Sunday you can try the events yourself—on
scaled-down versions, of course.

For those who prefer a bit more grace with their athletics, there's Scottish country dancing throughout the day, both Saturday and Sunday. The highlight of the weekend is the Ceilidh (*KAY-lee*), a Saturday night sing-a-long that blends voices with a pipe band.

For information send an email to info@kyscottishweekend. org. Or write Kentucky Scottish Weekend, Inc., P.O. Box 11441, Cincinnati, Ohio 45211-0441.

TOY TRAIN FESTIVAL
Carrollton

We love our trains in Kentucky. There's the Kentucky Railway Museum in New Haven and My Old Kentucky Dinner Train in Bardstown; the Elkhorn City Railroad Museum in Elkhorn City and the David A. Zegeer Coal-Railroad Museum in Jenkins; and the Bluegrass Railroad Museum in Versailles and this festival and swap meet for toy train aficionados in Carrollton. But let's tell the truth now. Amtrak doesn't stop in Kentucky.

We love our trains, but we don't have a passenger train stop. Okay, technically we do. The Kentucky Cardinal, which used to end its run in Jeffersonville, Indiana, now runs another mile across the Ohio for a daily stop in Louisville. But that was added in late 2001. For twenty years Kentucky was without any passenger train service.

But we do have the Toy Train Festival, which attracts grownup little boys from all over the country. You'll see everything from classic Lionel models to modern favorites like Thomas—and a swap meet like no other. At the end of the weekend many of the train enthusiasts head to nearby La Grange to watch the train go through the middle of the city. Now that's excitement.

For information on the Toy Train Show call (502) 743–5414.

POP. 28 — KENTUCKY'S SMALLEST TOWN
Concord

If you are old enough to recognize the names George Maharis and Martin Milner, then you know about Concord, the first stop for Maharis and Milner on their sixties TV drama *Route 66*. The first episode of the show was filmed in Concord, and the tiny town has been grateful ever since. But all that publicity couldn't turn the tide. Concord has been withering on the vine for more than half a century, and in the latest census it finally fell to the bottom: It is officially Kentucky's smallest town.

There may be communities with a smaller population than twenty-eight, but none is a bona-fide city, incorporated and a dues-paying member of the Kentucky League of Cities. Concord has a mayor and a town council; in fact the governing group comprises 20 percent of the town's residents.

Concord is shrinking despite the fact that it now has its own grocery store, Mary McClurg's Concord Little Country Store, which reopened in the mid-nineties. (McClurg told the Associated Press that she has to sell everything from foodstuffs to antiques to stay afloat; business is best when there's a funeral in town.)

In the 1990 census, Concord had sixty-five residents. It shrank by more than half in the decade of the nineties. Ah, but it had its glory days. When the town was incorporated in 1830, it boasted three hotels, a boarding house, a drug store, a sawmill, a doctor, and a lawyer.

Things have been downhill in the Lewis County community since the flood of '84, that's 1884, swept away most of First Street. The famous Ohio River flood of 1937 swallowed the rest of that lane—twenty-eight houses—and sent the town into a downward spiral.

Aside from McClurg's store there's not much else left in town: two churches and City Hall. That small population means a small tax base. When the city coffers are bare, Mayor Lovell Polley dips into his own pocket to pay the City Hall electric bill.

ONLY REPLICA OF THE TOMB OF JESUS IN THE U.S.
Covington

You don't have to go all the way to the Holy Land to see the tomb where Jesus was buried. You can visit Covington and see the only replica in this country. The Garden of Hope is modeled on Jerusalem's Garden Tomb, one of several Middle Eastern sites that are considered possibilities for Jesus's final resting place.

The idea for the tomb came from local TV evangelist Morris H. Coers, who visited the real site in 1938 and returned to America determined to built a duplicate. It took him almost a quarter century, but the Garden of Hope was officially dedicated on Easter Sunday 1960. Sadly the Reverend Coers didn't live to see the formal dedication; he died two months earlier.

The Reverand Coers was a stickler for details. He contracted with Solomon Mattar, caretaker of Jerusalem's Garden Tomb, to provide drawings of the Israeli site. Coers even flew Mattar in to put on the finishing touches. The garden includes stones imported from the Jordan River, the Wailing Wall, and Solomon's Temple. When it was finished, the Reverand Coers proclaimed the replica so accurate that even the interior echo sounded the same as the original.

But without its benefactor, the Garden of Hope fell on hard times. In the mid-nineties an anonymous benefactor paid off the garden's debt, and a committee from Coer's old church, Immanuel Baptist, oversaw a renovation that has the garden back to its original grandeur.

*Thanks to television evangelist Morris H. Coers, you don't have to go
all the way to the Holy Land to see the tomb where Jesus was
buried—or at least a replica of it.*

The Garden of Hope is located at 699 Edgecliff Drive just off
Sixteenth Street. For information call (859) 491–1777.

WORLD'S LARGEST HAND-BLOWN STAINED-GLASS CHURCH WINDOW
Covington

If you get up close, where you can't see the surrounding city,
and squint, it's like a miniature Notre Dame. Except of course
that no amount of urban renewal could make you think that
Covington is Paris.

The world's largest hand-blown stained-glass window—
67 feet high and 24 feet wide—is just one of eighty-two
that adorn the Cathedral Basilica of the Assumption.

The cathedral does have its own claim to world fame: It houses the largest hand-blown stained-glass church window in the world. The cathedral's north transept window, which depicts the fifth-century Ecumenical Council of Ephesus that proclaimed Mary as the Mother of God, is 67 feet high and 24 feet wide. All told, the church has eighty-two stained-glass windows.

The church is actually a copy of three famous French chapels: The exterior comes from the Abbey Church of Saint-Denis in Paris, the three-tiered interior walls are copied from Notre Dame de Chartres, and the facade is a one-third-scale replica of Cathedral de Notre Dame in Paris.

The cathedral is one of thirty-five minor basilicas in the United States and is home to the Roman Catholic Diocese of Covington. And here's a secret: The cathedral has never been completed, construction stopped in 1915.

The Cathedral Basilica of the Assumption is located at 1140 Madison Avenue.

FATHER OF SCOUTING FATHERED IN KENTUCKY
Covington

Daniel Carter Beard, or "Uncle Dan" as he is known to millions of men and young boys around the world, was born and raised in Covington—scout's honor!

Born in 1851, Beard, founding father of the American Boy Scouts, grew up camping and hiking in the wooded areas of Kentucky. He was deeply fascinated by tales of Daniel Boone and frontiersmen—he was only fifty or so years removed from those frontier days—spending hours recreating their experiences.

Beard was an environmentalist at heart, although he did set out to pursue a career in civil engineering and surveying. His passions were refocused, though, when outdoor and nature magazines began publishing illustrations he had drawn. Beard left engineering and never looked back.

The Boy Scouts were an organization formed in England. Stemming in part from his admiration for what the Brits were doing in teaching environmentalism to children, and in part from a desire to pass on his childhood experiences to kids who might not have access to nature and the outdoors, Beard formed the Boy Scouts of America in 1910. He also served as the first National Commissioner of the Boy Scouts, designed the uniforms, served as president of the Campfire Girls, formed the Society of the Sons of Daniel Boone, and wrote what is considered to be the definitive environmentalist manual, *The American Boy's Handy Book,* which has been in continuous publication for one hundred years. Whew! The *Handy Book* continues to be the bible of the Boy Scouts to this day.

Beard also illustrated many books, including the first edition of Mark Twain's *A Connecticut Yankee in King Arthur's Court.* Mt. Beard, adjoining Mt. McKinley, is named for him. Scout's honor.

Daniel Carter Beard Environmental Center is at 322 East Third Street in Covington. For information call (859) 261–3882.

FANTASY SUITES
Florence

In Florence you can visit the Old West, a stock car race, and the fifties—all without leaving the hotel grounds. Sound like a fantasy? That's what it's supposed to be. The Wildwood Inn offers a half dozen or so fantasy suites for visitors who want more than just a clean bed and cable TV.

For cowboys there's the Western Suite, with a poker table, an Old West–style bar, and an iron bed. For authenticity you pump your water; there are no spigots.

For Neanderthals there's the Cave Suite, with stalactites and stalagmites and a waterfall in the spa.

For a small price, you and your
honey can rev your engines in the racecar room.

Sleep like an Egyptian. A room fit for a king—
King Tut, that is—awaits you at the Wildwood Inn.

For sailors there's the Nautical Suite, with sleeping quarters in a boat.

For lovers there's the Cupid Suite, complete with a heart-shaped spa and a room decor that is heavy on the red.

For NASCAR fans there's the Pit Spa, with a racecar in the middle of the room and a Craftsman tool-caddy dresser.

And for fans of the fifties there's the Happy Days Suite, with a Cadillac bed (honest, the bed is inside a 1959 Caddy convertible), a ten-cent soft drink machine, and an Elvis figurine that shakes its hips to "Jail House Rock."

Yes, fantasy is the Wildwood's stock-in-trade. If you just want a clean bed and cable TV, the Wildwood has one hundred regular rooms, too.

The Wildwood Inn is at 7809 U.S. 42, just of I–75 at exit 180. Call (859) 371–6300 for information.

WORLD'S SMALLEST CHURCH
Fort Mitchell

Perhaps you remember the *Newhart* episode where Bob Newhart's character, Dick Loudon, was host of a local TV talk show and the day's guest had been billed as the world's smallest horse. "How do you know he's the world's smallest horse?" Dick earnestly asked the owner. "Well, look at him," the cowboy replied.

You'll also have to accept on faith, as it were, that the Monte Casino Chapel in Fort Mitchell is the world's smallest church. But look at it! It's 6 feet by 9 feet, just enough room for two worshippers. And that's a snug fit. The chapel, on the campus of Thomas More College, has been featured in "Ripley's Believe It or Not" as the World's Smallest Church, so what more validation could you want?

Sunday service at Monte Casino Chapel is always standing room only—as there's only room for two worshippers.

Why would someone build a church this small? The chapel was originally constructed as a sort of convenient prayer station for monks who worked in the vineyards that once stood here.

The world's smallest church, the Monte Casino Chapel, is located on the campus of Thomas More College. The college is on Turkey Foot Road, just south of I–275.

WORLD'S LONGEST YARD SALE

*I*n the pecking order of bargain hunting, it's the lowest—a notch below the flea market and several rungs down from the antiques auction. But the yard sale has its devotees, and every August they gather on a 450-mile stretch of U.S. 127 that runs from Covington all the way to Gadsden in northern Alabama to find those ultimate bargains.

And bargains there are: You can find anything from an antique oil painting to a used rake. There are car parts, music tapes, antiques, folk art, serious art, crafts—well, everything. There are as many different types of merchandise as there are vendors, and there are a lot of those—an estimated 3,500 tables and tents alongside the road.

It's a four-day yard sale, and veterans of the trek say there's no possible way to cover it all in four days. That's why the truly serious sneak out on Sunday, four days before the actual kickoff, and scour the merchandise even while the merchants are carting it out of the basement. The idea for the highway sale started with former Fentress County, Tennessee, official Mike Walker. He just wanted to get travelers off the interstate and into his county to do a little shopping. But the yard sale quickly took on a life of its own, jumping from a few dozen roadside vendors to a few thousand.

Traffic slows to a standstill in the more congested areas. That's because the event typically draws 20,000 cars. That's 20,000 more than the highway normally carries. If you can't find it at this yard sale, you don't need it.

The Fentress County (Tennessee) Chamber of Commerce coordinates the event. For information call (931) 879–9948.

BRICK SHOT—

John Wooden's Only Coaching Failure

*J*ohn Wooden was the greatest coach in the history of collegiate basketball. There's no argument even. He won more college basketball championships, ten, than any other coach. That's more than his closest rivals combined. His UCLA teams were legendary. They once won eighty-eight games in a row and had a stretch of seven consecutive NCAA tournament championships between 1967 and 1973.

But he wasn't always so successful. In fact, when Wooden started his coaching career at Dayton High School, his teams were not very good. He coached only two seasons there, but his record was a middling 21–14, including a losing season—a reported 8–9—in 1933–34. It was his only losing season in more than forty years of coaching.

In Wooden's defense he was little busy those two years, coaching all the school's athletic teams while teaching English and Phys. Ed. and adapting to his newlywed status—all on $150 a month. He left Dayton after the 1934 season to coach at South Bend Central in his native Indiana. In eleven years coaching high school basketball, his teams won 218 games while losing only 42. One-third of his losses were during those two years in Kentucky.

DUMMIES FOR DUMMIES
Fort Mitchell

Gone are the days of Ed Sullivan and Steve Allen, and with them are gone the regular national venues for "vents." Vent is short for ventriloquist, and in the days of Sullivan's *Toast of the Town,* performers who could throw their voices were a regular attraction. Now about the only place to enjoy the art is at Vent Haven, the only museum in America dedicated exclusively to ventriloquism.

Vent Haven is home to nearly 600 dummies—"dolls," vents prefer to call them—some of them more than a century old. The museum was the brainchild of Cincinnati businessman W. S. Berger, whose actor-father introduced him to the craft when he was a boy. Berger didn't get serious about collecting vent memorabilia until after his retirement from the presidency of the Cambridge Tile Co. in 1947. But when he got serious, boy, did he get serious. In addition to the variety of dummies, there are films, sheet music, props, and an 800-book library of ventriloquism manuals and joke books.

Among the inductees to the museum's Vent's Hall of Fame are Edgar Bergen, Shari Lewis, Paul Winchell, and Señor Wences. The museum doesn't have the most famous vent doll of all time, Bergen's Charlie McCarthy—that one is in the Smithsonian—but it has does have a detailed replica made especially for Vent Haven with the permission of Bergen's widow, Frances.

Vent Haven, 33 West Maple Avenue, is open only during the summer and only by appointment. The highlight of the museum's season is the annual international ConVENTion at the nearby Drawbridge Estate. For information call (859) 341-0461.

GARY BURBANK—
Barbecue Prophet

*H*e's not from Kentucky, and he doesn't currently work in Kentucky. But he lives in Kentucky, in the northern Kentucky town of Alexandria. His afternoon radio show on Cincinnati's 50,000-watt radio station, WIW, reaches all over the state. And from his many years on Louisville's WAKY and WHAS radio, many Kentuckians still think of them as their own.

He's Gary Burbank, a radio legend, the man behind—or rather the voice within—the syndicated radio comedy character Earl Pitts. Earl is red of neck and proud of it. Each weekday Earl's comments about things un-American are broadcast on some 200 stations all over the country. One day Earl told his listeners how they could tell if a redneck had been working on his computer: if the monitor is up on blocks, if the six front keys have rotted out, or if the password is "Bubba."

Burbank is a barbecue connoisseur, with three restaurants of his own in the Cincinnati area. He started the chain after being unable to find good barbecue to satisfy his Memphis-born palate. "They don't know what barbecue is in Cincinnati," contends Burbank. "Some people here took me to this place they said had the best barbecue in the country, and the waitress brought me something that looked like it had grape jelly on it. I told her to take it out and give it to the poor."

POPULATION
CENTER OF 1880

T *he exact center of the population of the United States*
in 1880 was located in Kentucky. In fact it was located
pretty much where the Cincinnati Airport is today. Of course
the population wasn't all that great in 1880—just 49,371,340
give or take a few souls.

What's that? You understand geographic center but wonder
what is the population center? Here's how demographers explained
it to me. Let's say everyone in the entire country weighed the same,
say 150 pounds. Then have everyone go home and sit for just one
second. Now peel up the country and put it on a needle. You'll
have to move the needle around, but when you get it to that
one spot where the country balances, that's the popula-
tion center.

When they took the 1880 census, that bal-
ancing spot was in Hebron, Kentucky—
where planes land today.

The Center of the Universe, circa 1880.

CINCINNATI, KENTUCKY
Hebron

L unken Airport, Cincinnati, Ohio's, international airport, is actually located in Kentucky. Oh, it wasn't always in Kentucky. At one time it was actually in Cincinnati, sitting on the city's eastern edge. But after the infamous 1937 Ohio River flood swamped the site, it became known as "Sunken Lunken," and Cincinnati began looking for a new site for its airport. It found it on a plateau 13 miles south of town, and in 1947 the first commercial airliner, a flight from Cleveland, landed at what was then Boone County Airport.

A 1948 flood at Sunken Lunken cinched the deal and Cincinnati's namesake airport has been in Kentucky ever since. And it's been a good deal. In 2001 the Cincinnati/Northern Kentucky International Airport was named Best Airport in the United States for passenger service and convenience in a survey by the International Air Transport Association.

The airport is located just off I–275, west of I–75.

FIRST TOWN NAMED FOR OUR FIRST PRESIDENT
Maysville

N o, the first president wasn't named Mays. It's just that Washington, Kentucky, is now a part of Maysville.

George Washington wasn't even president when the town was named in his honor in 1780. He was still a blue-collar general, fighting the British up and down the East Coast, trying to win independence for the Colonies. Cornwallis didn't surrender until the next year, and Washington didn't become president until 1789. By that time, his namesake town, home to 119 log cabins, was the second largest town in the state. Okay, technically Kentucky wasn't a state yet either. But Washington was the second largest town in the area that would become the state of Kentucky.

So the townspeople jumped the gun a little, hoping that the thriving little town would be named the capital of the soon-to-be United States. It didn't happen, of course. In fact it was probably a little cheeky to name a town for a rebel general while a war was still going on.

Washington did become a happening village for a time. It was a fashion center in the last years of the eighteenth century, with twenty stores, ten mechanics shops, three churches and two—count 'em, two—taverns. Despite the town's whistling and pulling up its skirt for attention, it never got the notice it wanted from the nation's father. George Washington never even slept here.

ROSEMARY CLOONEY MUSIC FESTIVAL
Maysville

What, no hot air balloon rides or 5K runs or antique tractors?

This unique festival is an annual celebration of the fact that Rosey could sing (something nephew George Clooney can't; his voice was dubbed for *O Brother Where Art Thou*). It's music, music, and more music.

Each September big-band legend Clooney would return to her hometown of Maysville from her Hollywood home for a concert to benefit the "Rescue the Russell" restoration project. The Russell is the Russell Theatre, a defunct movie house in downtown Maysville. The Russell had a special place in Clooney's heart. It's where she had the world premiere for her first film, *The Stars Are Singing*, in 1953.

Rosey and musical guests (one year it was Michael Feinstein, another it was daughter-in-law Debby Boone) would perform under the stars in the middle of Maysville's historic district. Clooney died in 2002, but the show will go on.

For ticket information—the event includes dinner—call (606) 564–9411.

THE GIFT SHOP THAT SOLD MORE FLORIDA SOUVENIRS THAN ANY GIFT SHOP NOT IN FLORIDA
Milton

Business is not what it used to be on U.S. 421 at the Kentucky-Indiana border—surely not what it was back in the fifties and sixties, when Route 421 was one of the main highways connecting the Midwest to Florida.

Then came I–75, which made the trip from Detroit to Miami fly by. It also made the tourists fly by. Once the interstate came, the business left—no more lines waiting to cross the Ohio River bridge. And with the interstate went one of the great distinctions in American business history. You see, before old I–75, the Kentucky Souvenir Shop in Milton, at the curve right before the bridge, was a tourist mecca. The tiny store sold more Florida souvenirs than any other gift shop not in Florida.

Go figure. Before the interstate was built, this little shop sold
more Florida souvenirs than any gift shop not in Florida.

A Kentucky gift shop located a souvenir ashtray's throw
from the Ohio River sold more Florida souvenirs than any gift
shop in America not in Florida? Sputter, choke, cough: How
could that be? Simple. People would get to the river, a few
hours from home, and remember what they forgot: to bring
back a souvenir from Florida.

Kentucky Souvenir stocked up on stuffed alligators, pink flamingo ashtrays, and Florida window decals. And it did gangbuster business. Then they built the interstate, and that was it—no more tourists, no more Florida souvenirs flying out the door. Now it's just a simple little souvenir shop.

Kentucky Souvenir Shop is at 12921 U.S. 421 North. For information call (502) 268-3374.

NEWPORT AQUARIUM
Newport

When most people think of Newport, they don't think of fish. Yeah, Newport is on the Ohio River, but the Ohio is not exactly a fisherman's paradise anymore. But Newport is home to one of the world's largest aquariums, what the advertising calls "one million gallons of fun." That's a lot of water.

Five local businessmen who love fish came up with the idea of an aquarium in 1990, but it took almost a decade to get the thing off the ground. (Well, it'll never be off the ground, not with a million gallons of water holding it down.) The aquarium finally opened in 1999 and is one of the most popular attractions in northern Kentucky—second only to where George Clooney kissed his first girl.

The aquarium is home to 11,000 marine animals, including fifty sharks and twelve penguins. Penguins and sharks in Kentucky? You gotta see it to believe it.

The aquarium is located on the Levee, a giant complex that includes retail stores and movie theaters, on Third Street, right on the Ohio River. Admission is $15.95 for adults, $9.95 for children. For more information call (859) 491–FINS (3467). FINS—that's cute.

WORLD'S LARGEST FREE-SWINGING BELL
Newport

Ooo-eee, is this exciting. Pack up the kids, Mildred, we're heading to the World's Largest Free-Swinging Bell. Okay, it may not sound all that exciting, but this is one serious bell: thirty-three tons, 12 feet high, and 12 feet wide. It's the most serious bell since that original serious bell, the Liberty Bell.

The World Peace Bell was built for the Millennium Moment, the turning of the twenty-first century. But it continues to ring loud and clear on special occasions, such as whenever its custodians decide to strike a note for world peace.

The bell is more than just a noisemaker; it's a sight. Its surface presents a sort of millennium's greatest hits: renderings of Columbus arriving in America, humans walking on the moon, Guttenberg creating movable type, Einstein figuring out his Theory of Relativity. The inscription on the bell reads: "The World Peace Bell is a symbol of freedom and peace, honoring our past, celebrating our present, and inspiring our future."

And since the bell is pretty new—cast in 1998—there's no crack, like that bell in Philadelphia.

The World Peace Bell is at the corner of Fourth and York Streets.

They call this 12-foot-high, 12-foot-wide, thirty-three-ton bell the Peace Bell. But how can there be any peace when that thing's ringing?

DOWN THE RABBIT HOLE TO
RABBIT HASH
Rabbit Hash

To get to the Rabbit Hash General Store, you have to want to get to the Rabbit Hash General Store. It's not on the way to anything; in fact they may well have coined the expression "out of the way" just to describe its location. Step inside and it's like stepping back in time. But what would you expect from a store that's been open since 1831.

The Rabbit Hash General Store's been open since 1831—though it does close now and then.

Sometimes that time seems more like the seventies—the 1970s, not the 1870s. Ask for a candy bar and you'll be offered an organic peanut butter cup. Ask for a soft drink and you'll be directed to the Coke case, where you can purchase Coca-Cola in an old-fashioned six-ounce bottle—that is if you can *get* to the Coke case. There's often a dog sleeping in front of it. The store may be untouched by time, but the Ohio River hasn't been so kind. The place was submerged during the floods of 1884, 1913, and 1937. There's still mud from the '37 flood in the attic.

In addition to snack food, the store sells antiques, crafts, postcards, and, my favorite item, the Rabbit Hash T-shirt, emblazoned with "Rabbit Hash Volunteer Fire Department, String Band, and S.W.A.T. Team."

Get off I-75 at the Big Bone Lick State Park exit and head west. Stay on Highway 536; you'll find it.

BIG BONE LICK STATE PARK
Union

Hee-hee-hee, he said "Big Bone Lick!" Fans of *Beavis and Butthead* know what I'm talking about. The slightly risqué name for this state park often raises eyebrows. We have a number of sites in Kentucky that end in "lick"—and stir up the sophomore in all of us.

But Big Bone Lick is actually a very important area. Twelve thousand years ago, mammals pushed south by Ice Age glaciers found this site, with its mineral waters and salt lick. On any given prehistoric day you could find mastodons and mammoths,

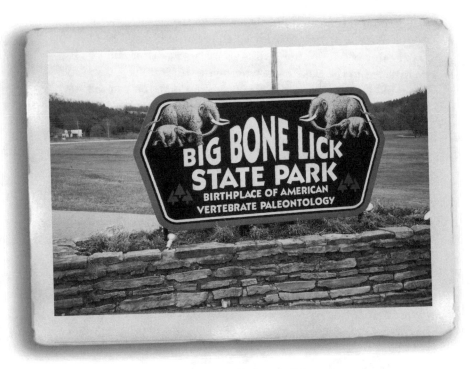

Yeah, yeah, it has a funny name. We know.
Get your laughs out now . . .

bison and ground sloths, shoulder to giant shoulder, basking in
the swampy waters and licking the salt. Some became trapped
in the marshes and died. Jump ahead to the 1700s, when early
settlers discovered these *mammoth* mammoth bones and established the science of Vertebrate Paleontology.

The park celebrates its past with both an indoor and an outdoor museum, plus a diorama depicting its Ice Age glory. You
can also camp, picnic, hike, and play miniature golf.

Big Bone Lick State Park is at 3380 Beaver Road. For information call (859) 384–3522.

E*AT* D*ESSERT* F*IRST*
Washington

Chocolate eggs. Hot chocolate. Chocolate bunnies. Chocolate pie.

Chocolate-covered cream candy. Chocolate cake. Chocolate chip cookies. Bourbon balls.

Turtles. Fudge. Bonbons. Toffee. Suckers.

Chocolate mousse. Chocolate pastry. Chocolate waffles. Chocolate ice cream.

Now that I have your attention, it's time to talk chocolate—and who doesn't want to talk about that subject? They've been celebrating the wonderful substance in Washington for more than a decade with the annual Chocolate Festival.

For the ridiculously low price of $5.00 you can walk through the old downtown sampling chocolate delights—now *that's* redundant—to your heart's content on handmade candies, homemade cakes, handmade cookies, homemade pies, and handmade fudge. And while you are gorging on all that sweet, delicious chocolate, you can feel good about yourself because you are helping a worthy cause: Hospice of Southern Kentucky.

Washington is 1 mile south of the AA Highway on U.S. 68. For information on the festival, held every March, call (606) 759-7423.

THE GHOST OF SPIRITS PAST
Wilder

Most "ghost" sites are proud to claim one sighting. But Bobby Mackey's Music World is the mother of all haunted houses—some call it The Most Haunted Place in America—with what must be a record twenty-nine ghostly appearances, all backed up by affidavits.

It didn't start out that way. The original building was a slaughterhouse with a well in the basement for blood to drain. It was the lower room that a satanic cult later chose for its regular rituals. On one occasion in 1896 that ritual allegedly involved the head of a Greencastle, Indiana, woman, Pearl Bryan, who was killed by her boyfriend and his pal after a botched abortion. The two were caught and convicted, but, fearing the wrath of Satan, they would not disclose the location of Pearl's missing head. On the gallows, the accused vowed he would come back and get his revenge on the townspeople who had condemned him. Legend has it that all the lawyers and judges involved in the case died untimely deaths.

During Prohibition the slaughterhouse was razed and replaced by a speakeasy, which eventually became a bar and casino known as Buck Brady's Primrose. But it, too, came to an unhappy end after Red Masterson, owner of the rival Merchant's Club, suggested that Buck might want to sell out and Buck gave his answer with a double-barreled shotgun. No charges were filed against Brady; Masterson lived but claimed that he couldn't identify his assailant. But something transpired, because soon Brady sold out to the Cleveland syndicate, which renamed the place the Latin Quarter. Sometime before The Quarter was shut down in the early sixties after a gambling raid, a club manager's daughter named Johanna committed suicide in the basement.

In 1970 the place morphed into a roadhouse called Hard Rock Cafe (no relation to the chain), which was shut down in 1978 after a series of fatal shootings. That's when Bobby and Janet Mackey purchased the building and turned it into a country music bar popular for its spirits of the alcoholic variety. But soon other spirits arrived. In the past two decades there have been reports of scary sounds, spooky sightings of a headless ghost (that would be Pearl Ryan), apparitions of angry men (probably her killers), and a spirit calling herself "Johanna."

Writer Doug Hensley has put this story together in great detail in his book *Hell's Gate*. Read it and you will believe.

Bobby Mackey's Music World is located at 44 Licking Pike in Wilder. For information call (606) 431–5588.

Back, by popular demand. Over the years there've been a record twenty-nine ghostly appearances at Bobby Mackey's Music World.

KENTUCKY BBQ

We love barbecue in Kentucky, so much so that we stage festivals all over the state honoring this wondrous food. These barbecue festivals can make for a lively weekend outing. They're also a great place for tasting great barbecue.

At most festivals, once the judging is over, the contestants start passing out free meat. All you have to do is stand in line. At others you may need to make friends. But that's easy enough. Barbecue cooks love to talk about their barbecue and their cooker.

You can find a barbecue festival somewhere just about every weekend during the summer.

Here are a few of the major ones.

MAY:	Bar-B-Q Pitt Festival, *Louisville's Pitt Academy*, (502) 966–6979
	Fountain Run Barbecue Festival, *Fountain Run*, (270) 434–4080
	International Bar-B-Q Festival, *Owensboro*, (270) 926–6938
JUNE:	W.C. Handy Blues & Barbecue Festival, *Henderson*, (800) 648–3128
	Microbrew and Bar-B-Q Festival, *Louisville's Churchill Downs*, (502) 636–4400
JULY:	Bar-B-Que and Homecoming, *Dawson Springs*, (270) 821–3435
SEPTEMBER:	Barbecue on the River & Old Market Days, *Paducah*, (270) 443–8783
OCTOBER:	Outdoor Expo and Barbecue Festival, *Madisonville*, (270) 821–3435

This *Jackelope-shaped* cooker made an appearance at the now-defunct Louisville Bar-B-Que Festival in 1987. Fun-looking cookers spotted at recent festivals include a riverboat-shaped cooker and a train-shaped cooker.

INDEX